Assessing Communication
Integrated Approaches in Political, Social and Business Context

Emiliana De Blasio
Enrico Gandolfi
Paolo Peverini
Elsa Pili
Mariacristina Sciannamblo
Donatella Selva
Noemi Trino

Edited by Michele Sorice

© 2012 Pola Srl a socio unico

All rights reserved. No part of this publication may be reproduced, stored in a retrieval system, or transmitted, in any form or by any means, electronic, mechanical, photocopying, recording, or otherwise, without the prior permission of Pola Srl.

ISBN 978-88-6105-132-4

LUISS University Press – Pola s.r.l.
Viale Pola, 12
00198 Roma

Phone: +39.06.85225.485
Email address: lup@luiss.it

www.luissuniversitypress.it

Table of contents

Preface 7
Pier Luigi Celli

Introduction 11
Michele Sorice

The problem of evaluating public relation activities as social
and intangible issues: the importance of research with
practical applications 15
Mariacristina Sciannamblo

Politics in the Web 2.0. Between trust and credibility 53
Emiliana De Blasio

What is the mud machine ("macchina del fango"):
genesis and development of a political use of media power. 63
Noemi Trino

Campbell, Blair and Iraq: how the spin doctor spun the spin 87
Elsa Pili

"If you do not believe it just ask them". The credibility
management of the Catholic Church in the 8x1000 campaigns 105
Paolo Peverini

The construction of credibility: a case study from television 123
Donatella Selva

Game on the press, between prejudice and technology 137
Enrico Gandolfi

Communication is business: the strategic role of intangible
assets in the process of reputation building. 153
Mariacristina Sciannamblo

Centre for Media and Communication Studies "Massimo Baldini"

Steering Committee

Director: Michele Sorice
Coordinator: Emiliana De Blasio

Members: Sergio Fabbrini, Matthew Hibberd, Paolo Peverini, Philip Schlesinger, Dario Edoardo Viganò

Scientific Advisory Board

President: Leonardo Morlino
Members: Pierpaolo Donati, David Forgacs, Guido Gili, Michael Higgins, Giuseppe Richeri, Michael Temple, Sofia Ventura

Contacts:

Centre for Media and Communication Studies "Massimo Baldini"
LUISS Guido Carli
Viale Romania 32
00197 Rome RM – Italy
Phone: +39.06.85225.759
Email address: communication@luiss.it
http://ricerca.scienzepolitiche.luiss.it/en/research-centers/centre-media-and-communication-studies

Preface

Pier Luigi Celli

In the 20th century scholars and professionals spoke of political propaganda, commercial advertising and public service announcements; in the 21st century we speak of political communication, corporate communication and social communication. The difference is not just semantic, it reflects a trend that has widened the scope, by converging the techniques and tools used. Technological progress, shortening the time to online messages and allowing significantly their expansion, has not only accelerated the communication process but it has also modified other communication fields such as news reporting.

In the last century, journalism was the result of the work of professionals who were neutral viewers; they had the task to tell the events, to comment and to search for the best balance among the expressed opinions. Today, journalists working in the frame of traditional media, seems overcame by the web competitors; then to preserve interest for their product, they have to go in the side of "comment", almost leaving the facts, with the natural effect to become communication sources themselves.

The main topic of this book is constituted by the analysis of the creation and preservation of reputation and credibility by different social actors in front of their reference audiences (the citizens as consumers, voters or even religious practitioner).

Mariacristina Sciannamblo focuses her research on the reputation in the business environment, with examples of specific cases; she also studies how to measure the required actions of public relations, trying to determine their effectiveness. She proceeds with a careful review of the entire doctrine on the topic, to evaluate different models, till the latest. And it is really satisfactory to observe that in an English-speaking and a predominantly Anglo-Saxon professional world, the author indicates an Italian method as the one offering the most positive development and, anyway, one of the most interesting.

Emiliana De Blasio's chapter is very important because it defines the theoretical frame concerning the relationship between political communication and the web 2.0. At the same time, the chapter represents the essential linkage between the 2010

CMCS research on media and credibility and this book. The relationship between credibility and trust constitutes an important shift of paradigm: from a media-centred perspective to a socio-centred perspective. The chapter also presents some tools (such as the so-called *buzz monitoring*) that can be used jointly with social research techniques but also with quantitative methods, becoming very helpful to understand how media can discredit companies and political actors.

Noemi Trino and Elsa Pili, using two different but close perspectives, study mediated political communication, also drawing how the media can become tools for behavior's influence. They use different case studies but it is not a case that changing only the social actors (an Italian newspaper from one side and a famous British politician with his spin-doctor from the other side) the final result is not so different. In another chapter, Donatella Selva tackles the issue of media credibility, studying the case of an Italian journalist and TV showman.

The complete cycle of communication actions and the consequences generated in terms of reputation, at this moment, can be evaluated only in the case of Tony Blair and Alastair Campbell because the period under review is long enough for an evaluation in terms of reputation. In the case of "Il Giornale" and Mr. Gianfranco Fini, this exercise is more difficult: we can certainly see that the newspaper, with what the author rightly calls the "mud machine" (Italian "macchina del fango"), failed to make the Parliament's President resign; but it is still unclear how, how much, to what extent and "if" the media strategy has been able to affect the credibility of Mr. Gianfranco Fini. An evaluation could be found (and only in very partially way) in the next general elections.

The case of participatory journalism by Michele Santoro, beyond his undeniable success in terms of audience, will be assessed objectively in terms of credibility only when the Italian period of radical communication opposition will became history.

Paolo Peverini traces, instead, the phenomenon of social communication and advertising campaigns concerning the so-called "eight per thousand" (the share of taxes that citizens can devolve to the religious confessions) of the Catholic Church, using a socio-semiotic reflection aimed to find meanings in the signs of continuing renegotiation of credibility, usually submitted to constant and vehement criticism.

The chapter written by Enrico Gandolfi offers a concrete example, in the business perspective, which seems to be in contrast with what other authors assert. Here the scaring and smearing communication by a magazine about a product has not only no negative impact but it can also generate curiosity and determines its promotion.

The merit of this collection of essays and studies conducted by the Centre for Media and Communication Studies "Massimo Baldini", directed by Michele Sorice and coordinated by Emiliana De Blasio, is, without any doubt, its interdisciplinary nature in a methodological convergence style. The approach to political communication, social communication and business communication is the same, only analysed topics change. It is significant that this methodological and disciplinary merging takes place in a book published by a university that has its historical roots in the two academic strands: politics and business. It seems like to anticipate a collaborative project and a common evolution of different social studies.

Introduction

Michele Sorice

The relationship between media and society represents a major theme in the social sciences and, in recent years, it is becoming very important for the political science too. The media (it means media institutions, individuals who are part of and popular culture) have kept a strong relationship with the society, to whom they belong. The media play an important role in contemporary societies and the "media institutions" are inside a very dense network of relationships. This concept is connected with the question of "power", one of the key aspects in the cultural studies approach (in particular in the frame represented by the Birmingham's Centre for Contemporary Cultural Studies, which has been very influential to create linkages between the media studies, the sociology of culture and the political communication).

One of the most studied mechanisms of media studies concerns the relationship between media institutions and audience. This mechanism applies to a specific power of the media, which covers the meaning's building and relates to the processes through which media texts (eg television programs, movies, information, etc.) produce "effects" and / or "influence" over the public sphere. The media effects study has been a very important topic in all field of media studies and, in particular, in US communication research (whose most influential author are Harold Lasswell, Paul F. Lazarsfeld, Elihu Katz and, in more articulated and original perspective, Robert K. Merton).

About the question of the media as instruments of "power" in the logic of construction of social meaning, Denis McQuail identifies two types of media power and six main features of it. The two types refer to the so-called models of hegemony and that of pluralism, while the six main characteristics of the media power are the following: 1) ability to attract and to direct public attention, 2) ability in persuasion in matters concerning opinions and beliefs, 3) ability to influence behavior, 4) ability to structure the mechanisms of reality definition; 5) ability to confer status and social acceptance; 6) ability to provide information quickly and broadly (Sorice, 2009).

Going beyond the theoretical frame, it is mandatory to underline how the media can play an important role in matters concerning opinions and beliefs and, of course, in processes through which people are legitimated (or not) as social actors. In this perspective, media can improve (or delegimate) personal and corporate credibility. Credibility is a very important topic we have discussed in previous works (Scandaletti, Sorice, 2010). It is important here to remind the important and innovative research about credibility and reputation in the internet presented, in that book, by Emiliana De Blasio (2010) and which constitutes one of our theoretical and methodological starting point.

The credibility is essentially an effect of meaning, and not an intrinsic moral quality of the sender. Guido Gili (2005) in this context identifies the relational character of the credibility; in other terms, it refers to a network of social expectations. In fact, we can speak of a screen credibility of a perceived credibility both rooted in three macro areas: a cognitive basis (concerning the skills), an ethical-evaluative foundation (concerning the values) and finally an affective-emotional foundation (concerning the perception of a positive relationship between sender and receiver/audience). These aspects are closely related to two important elements such as distance and involvement.

Credibility presents some characteristics, usually referred to "credible source": integrity (also mentioned by Aristotle), the earnestness-reliability and consistency, which can also be defined as forms of loyalty. Obviously the source is credible if it has - at least in connection with its audience - fairness and independence, two features that are often required to journalism, even if not always pursued by the media companies and often requested by the public only as a matter of principle. Among the features that justify the credible source, Guido Gili still identifies the spontaneity and sympathy, dimensions that often represent the reasons for the success of the spectacular information.

The credibility, finally, is also a "transferable value"; in this respect one can not but note that the credibility of management inevitably leads to consensus-building and, more generally, in the news management, where even in a more evident way (and sometimes not without practical and ethical problems) emerges the relational dimension of credibility.

After two years from our first research on credibility in the news, we have decided to study how credibility crosses the social and corporate reputation. In 2010 we published a research about the credibility of media system; now we have reversed the perspective, investigating how the media system can improve or destroy credibility and reputation.

From a methodological point of view, our choice, in this case, has been that to realize specific coring in the huge field of information and communication. So we have put under analysis some cases of corporate, social and political credibility and reputation. The basic questions were: a) how does the media system influence personal or corporate credibility? What happens when a social actor (companies, journalists, politicians) is subjected to the "negativization" (Sorice, 2011) of his/her image because of the media coverage? What are the tools that public relations can use to reverse the negative trend or strengthen the positive one? How can we evaluate the quality of communication?

We do not pretend to respond comprehensively to all these questions, which together constitute abroad research program, also needed of many resources. So we defined our attention to some cases. At the same time, we have examined different methods and tools, both quantitative and qualitative; methodologies coming from the tradition of public relations or typical of the social sciences, semiotics approaches and consolidated analytical tools of the political communication.

The emerging picture is composite and articulated: and, for this reason, extraordinarily interesting. It represents a first step in a field of study that will require further research and other case studies to investigate.

REFERENCES

De Blasio, E. (2010) "Informazione e social media. Fra credibilità, fiducia e nuove intermediazioni", in Scandaletti, P., Sorice, M. eds. (2010) *Yes, credibility. La precaria credibilità del sistema dei media.* Roma: UCSI Unisob CDG.

Gili, G. (2005) *La credibilità. Quando e perché la comunicazione ha successo.* Soveria Mannelli: Rubbettino.

Scandaletti, P., Sorice, M. eds. (2010) *Yes, credibility. La precaria credibilità del sistema dei media.* Roma: UCSI Unisob CDG.

Sorice, M. (2009) *Sociologia dei mass media.* Roma: Carocci.

Sorice, M. (2011) *La comunicazione politica.* Roma: Carocci.

The Problem of Evaluating Public Relation Activities As Social And Intangible Issues: The Importance of Research With Practical Applications

Mariacristina Sciannamblo

"Which is the Return on Investment (ROI) from Public Relations (PR) activities?" "Why don't most senior management take PR as seriously as other company disciplines?". These common questions well explain the so-called 'PR dilemma' as the most pressing problem that affects PR practitioners all over the world. The difficulty of quantifying the actual PR value has been very often expressed by both professionals and academic researchers since all activities conducted by profit-making organizations have to be measured and made accountable against their set objectives. "If you cannot measure your activities, that means you cannot manage them": the senior management always keeps up this numerical mind set at heart. As Jim Macnamara (2008) argues, the struggle for legitimacy of any management discipline or practice focuses on demonstration that it adds value to the field it seeks to serve. Accordingly, in today's efficiency business world, if any activity does not add value, it is likely to be eliminated. Moreover, demonstrating results usually means quantifying the value added.

To better understand the issue, it could be useful trying to provide an exhaustive definition of the subject. According to James Grunig, PR has to enhance good relationships between the company and the public in order to promote its trust, commitment and satisfaction. Therefore, to the most professionals, PR deals with human beings, perceptions, feelings, prejudices, which are not easily measurable. But the logic underlying company organizations is made up of the relationship between benefits and costs: if benefits exceed costs, the programme sounds good. Accordingly, PR, as the other counterparts, has to create more benefits than costs as well as points out tangible results.

Despite there are still many professionals refusing to treat PR as a quantifiable activity, there is no doubt that it is definitely possible to measure its effectiveness. Furthermore, determining PR results has become increasingly important both to communication professionals and to the greater business community.

According to AMEC (The International Association for the Measurement and Evaluation of Communication), "media evaluation is a strategic and tactical tool for people working within PR, marketing or business intelligence". In 2004, the *Communications Executive Council* (CEC) conducted a survey of hundreds of chief communication officers in major corporations which points out that the 79% of the respondents believed communication performance measurement was more important than it had been three years before (Argenti, 2006).

Despite the increased usage of research in PR, recent studies in the US and UK show that a majority of PR professionals still implement programs and activities with totally inadequate research, strategies and results (Macnamara, 2006). Consequently, there is no surprise if research shows that the lack of measurement has negative effects on PR and corporate communication in terms of budgets, status and acceptance (Macnamara, 2006).

According to the Institute for Public Relations *Guidelines for Measuring and Evaluating PR effectiveness* (2002), "PR measurement and evaluation involves assessing the success or failure of specific PR programs, strategies, activities or tactics by measuring the *outputs, out-takes and/or outcomes* of those programs against a predetermined set of objectives". In the long-term, it involves the success or failure of PR efforts to improve and enhance the relationships with key players.

More specifically, PR measurement is used to give result a precise dimension, generally by comparison to some standard or baseline and usually is done in a quantifiable or numerical manner whereas *PR evaluation* determines the *value* or importance of a PR program or effort, usually through appraisal or comparison with a predetermined set of organization goals and objectives.

Despite the common agreement about the requirement for PR measurement, not everyone in the communications industry views the issue in the same light. As Paul A. Argenti (2006) illustrates, there is a dichotomy indicating the different points of view among corporate communications professionals: while some of them embrace the science of measurement as it relates to communications, others look at PR as an art outside the realm of formal measurement.

A study with practical applications cannot leave aside the reasons why measurement is important:

- It enables communication professionals to meet demands from senior managers;
- It justifies the budget;
- It allows to set more effective communication strategies.

As Paul Argenti (2006) argues, "in many cases, companies do not require more or better measurement, only better use of existing measurement data". In this regard, the ability of understanding how PR activities affect business outcomes will have a greater effect on business results going forward rather than simply justifying what they have done in the past.

The current methods of measuring PR in common use range across a variety of disciplines, subject area and depth of research (Blowers, 2006). On the one hand, we find traditional quantitative media research, that measure column inches and advertising value equivalent: these techniques have been around for many years until it became necessary to replace them with more sophisticated ones.

On the other hand, there are PR departments that undertake integrated research programs, both quantitative and qualitative. With regard to the latter, there is a broad range of media analysis projects known as *media content analysis* which consists in the evaluation of media data using a number of metrics (quantitative and qualitative), involving the analysis of message and *favourability*. Message analysis often comes in two forms: specific messages and other, relevant messages (negative, responsive etc).

Favourability is another qualitative measure, commonly applied with the use of categories of "positive", "neutral" and "negative" (Blowers, 2006).

An editorial in *PR Week* made the point about media metrics requirement (see Argenti, 2006):

"Business leaders are interested in investing capital in activities and assets for which they risk and return characteristics can be objectively measured, analyzed, and predicted with some degree of certainty based on data and facts. If intangibles like chemistry and creativity are positioned as the deciding factors, then PR looks more like a leap of faith than a good investment".

As Chang Peng Kee (2006) states, there is no perfection in any single method or tool in measuring PR effectiveness even if different organizations would like to have their unique approach on media evaluation. The media coverage debate concerns, above all, the different methods used to define the return on expenditure (ROE) of media campaigns. These methods of measuring PR range across a variety of disciplines and subjects and approaches.

According to Peng Kee, the media coverage debate begins since the *Advertising Value Equivalency* (AVE) was mooted. This method consists of evaluating media exposure (type, space, position) and the corresponding advertising rate in order to assign a monetary value to every PR news according to the outlays for advertising activities. Other quantitative methods are the *Opportunities To See* (OTS), used by advertisers to determine the position and to reach their products, and *Cost Per Mille* (CPM), derived by taking a said expenditure to multiply by a thousand and then divided by the total news impression.

The requirement for PR measurement and its effects on business results is faced up entirely by the second European summit on Measurement in PR (2010), organized by the *International Association for Measurement and Evaluation of Communication* (AMEC) and the *Institute for Public Relations* (IPR). "The importance of goal setting and measurement" and "the effect on business results can and should be measured where possible" are two of the seven principles for measuring and evaluating of PR set out. Goals address who, what, when, and how much is expected from a public relations campaign.

Despite the obstacles, once the link between communication activities and business outcomes is clear the communications industry and businesses will reap great benefits such as more respect for communications professionals, greater control over communications efforts, increase funding and, therefore, better business outcomes.

As the last studies point out, PR have to utilize research methodologies such as feedback, interviews, surveys, focus groups, case studies and pre-testing to evaluate outputs and outcomes like relationships and open "two-way" dialogue with partner relationship (customers, employees, shareholders, communities). The use of credible methods will be aid PR for a greater acceptance within the company and a higher budget and respect as it provides proof to support decisions and investments.

One of the main interesting insight into media studies (Blowers, 2006) is that PR operates not only in the financial area but also in company's environment and its community performance: many studies point out that getting one wrong has implications for the others. Accordingly, the Return on Investment of PR has to concern some other factors (Macnamara, 2003) such as employee motivation, relations with government and regulators, relations with non-governmental organizations and financial community, positive media coverage, supportive and loyal shareholders, well informed consumers and relationships with local communities.

PUBLIC RELATION THEORY: STATE OF THE RESEARCH

In 2001, James Grunig, one of the first and main practitioner and researcher in public relation field, warned both scholars and practitioners about the need to rethink public relations: "in a professional field such as public relations, I believe scholars must go beyond criticizing theories; they also have the obligation to replace theories with something better – an obligation that many critical scholars do not fulfill". This comment is indicative of a need for critical researchers and theorists to more clearly outline how their approaches contribute to advance not only public relations theory, but also research and practice.

Problems arisen between the world of academics and professionals in public relation research concern their own specific role: professionals are interested in short-term research, aiming to show the contribution of public relations in terms of general effectiveness of the organization whereas academics are more critical because of their role. However, if researchers do not think theoretically before measuring something, they will not achieve useful or valid results.

As Grunig (2006) points out, in spite of progress made in the last forty years, the public relations profession is still far from being a research-based profession. One of the main problem is to find a good balance between the quality of research and its conceptual efficacy: too often, research is conducted only to justify the money spent on public relations programs, trying to prove that publicity in the media has its own value or that public relations should get more of the money that goes to advertising in marketing communication plans. Seldom, research is done to plan public relations programs or to improve them and seldom research is used as a form of communication to bring information from publics into management decision-making process (Grunig, 2006).

Building a basic conceptual foundation is the first and essential step in order to conduct a research with valid results: if researchers do not think in theoretical terms firstly, it is likely to turn out to have little or invalid results in their measurements. Thus, it becomes necessary to define problems and to identify variables (dependent and independent) that can be changed, then determining if the problem has been solved. In other words, it need to develop a specific conceptualization in order to be able to explain why is doing, what is doing or which are the effects (Grunig, 2006).

In order to conceptualize public relation practices, we argue that it is unavoidable to consider political, economic and social contexts in which they operate. Moreover, considering the wider cultural context of public relations practice enables researchers to fully theorize how publics are encouraged to conceptualize "the public interest" and support the public relations message (Motion & Weaver, 2005). The value of this critical approach is aimed to investigate how political, sociocultural and economic conditions are able to shape the public relations practice and to determine the *power* and *influence* it presumes to yield through the practice.

To understand how PR promotes selected positions of truth and power, we have to examine the discourses and strategies deployed by practitioners. These are deployed to influence public opinion and achieve political, economic and sociocultural transformation.

As Fairclough (1992) explained, discourse is "a practice, not just of representing the world, but of signifying the world in meaning"; thus, observing public relations goals and practices, we can say that their main role is to provide and to shape the meanings for social, cultural political and economic experiences to benefit the client organization. In this view, the term 'power' carries on a positive and productive connotation as Foucault (1969; 1972) had noticed. From this perspective then, discourse is the vehicle through which power and truth circulate and it is also the mean by which public relations practitioners attempt to strategically maintain and to reproduce the existing state or to transform society (Motion & Weaver, 2005).

So, within this theoretical architecture it is possible to bring critical analysis of public relations. In this sense, the value of researching and theorizing the social and political implications of communication practice becomes clear and remarkable.

In public relations reflection, concepts such as 'image', 'reputation', 'brand', 'relationships' and 'issues' are the most common and they can be considered as outcomes of behaviors and processes that can be changed. According to Grunig (2006), "a logical conceptualization of the public relations process states that public relations people manage *communication* with *top managers* and with *publics* to contribute to the strategic decision processes of organizations. They manage communication between management and publics to build *relationships* with the publics that are most likely to affect the behavior of the organization or who are most affected by the behavior of the organization". So communication processes can be changed as they can be considered an independent variable together with management behaviors; these two variables have direct influence on key elements such as relationships above all, reputations, images, attitudes and brands. We cannot forget that these variables are also affected by other ones outside the control of public relations such as finance, economy and corporate behaviors (Grunig, 2006).

Researchers have to operate with these patterns choosing two level of analysis: formative research to formulate theories and evaluative research to pretest and post-test what the formative one has conceptualized. The formative research, indeed, develops programs, structures, organizational policies and behaviors that the other one implements.

Before to explain how public relations can make the organizations more effective, it is necessary to understand what it means for an organization to be effective. We could say that profitable and good organizations are those ones that achieve their goals; but, prior to plan strategies, organizations have to determine which goals are most important. They have to choose goals that are valued by their publics both inside and outside in order to become effective. Furthermore, it is important to develop good relationships aiming to achieve management, public and stakeholders support. It is peculiar duty of a public relations department to set up the most strategic public and conduct communication programs to develop long-term relationships with counterparts. In this way, according to Grunig, we should be able to determine the value of PR activities by measuring the quality of relationships with strategic publics.

To better evaluate the effectiveness of PR programs, we consider four higher units of analysis, whose effectiveness contributes to the effectiveness of the others. They are: the program level, the functional level, the organizational level, the societal level (Grunig, 2006). The *program level* refers to individual communication programs such as media relations, community relations, customer relations or employee relations that are components of the overall public relations function of an organization. This kind of programs usually set up specific goals such as affecting the cognitions, attitudes and behaviors of both publics and members of the company and they subsequently affect relationships between the organization and publics.

The *functional level* considers the overall PR function of an organization, so it considers different communication programs for different publics. At this level, the focus of analysis concerns how the public relations function is integrated into the overall management processes and how well PR practitioners have chosen appropriate publics and objectives for individual programs. Thus, it becomes necessary that PR departments compares its programs and processes with those of similar departments in other organizations.

In this way, what is evaluated is the quality of integration between organization's goals and expectations and needs of its strategic publics. The problem at this point, as we are going to see in the following pages, is that the value of this contribution is often not completely measurable in monetary terms because the added value, in this case, concerns human relationships.

Finally, we can consider the societal level, which refers to evaluation of the contribution that organization makes to the overall welfare of society as it is possible to know, through social responsibility, review and report. Ethical behavior and social responsibility are the two patterns considered at this level where also PR plays its role in order to build a socially responsible organization.

As for the state of research, several scholars recognize public relations as both a professional practice and a sub field of communication with its own research and theory base (Botan & Taylor, 2004). At the same time, this field has been developed as a theoretical area of applied communication in only the last about 25 years. There are some problems dealing with the *relationship* between industry and academy in defining a more or less precise concept that we can call 'public relations' (Hatherell & Bartlett, 2005): if, on the one hand, public relations is at a crucial point in explicating its central tasks and focus on the path to professionalism, on the other hand this situation impedes discussion within the academic community about defining the boundaries of the base knowledge. Literature (Grunig & Huang, 2000) identifies at least six model (persuasion, advocacy, public information, cause-related public relations, image/reputation management, relationship management) of which PR executives have to deal with. Furthermore, even though PR is considered a type of applied communication, it is often understood only as a technical area; therefore, PR academic faculties are screened for technical skills and are often not expected to have researchers and theorists.

According to Botan and Taylor (2004), the most noticeable trend in public relations over the past 20 years is its transition from a functional perspective to a cocreational one. The first one, prevalent in the early years of the PR field, considers publics and communication as tools or means useful to achieve organizational goals. The main activity is that one of founding valid techniques in order to set up strategic organizational messages, underlying only one kind of relationship: the one between PR practitioner and media. This approach of research is evidently far from the relational approach analyzed by Ferguson in 1984 as it has traditionally been concerned with business-oriented topics such as advertising, marketing and media relations. This functional perspective, followed by scholarship for many years, focuses on the use of PR as an instrument to accomplish specific organizational goals rather than on relationships. It is gathered, indeed, that public relations theory is very close to a pragmatic practice and, therefore, to utilitarian theories.

Since theoretical issues have affected public relations field, it is expanding beyond a mere functional perspective toward a view that focuses on communication as a meaning-making process. Botan and Taylor (2004) define this new approach "co-creational", underlying the role of publics as "co-creators" of meaning and what makes possible to share meanings, interpretations and goals. This perspective is long term in its orientation and focuses on relationships among publics and organizations. If we were to find a theoretical ground picked up from media studies we would mention the so called "dialogue theories" (Sorice, 2010), which imply the renewed role of the audience, no more considered as means to an end but instead as active partners in the meaning-making process.

Within the perspective of media studies, these theoretical formulations (Moores, 2005; Sorice 2000, 2005) focus on social subjects compared to the systems and on the importance of context within the publics activate social practices. In this path, publics are the defining force in the "cocreation" issues as relational approaches explain. This field of study (Broom, Casey, Ritchey, 1997; Grunig & Huang 2000) focuses on explication, operationalizing and measuring relationships. Among other theory bases used, public relations scholars have revisited interpersonal communication to understand relationship building better, including the construct of trust, often seen as an important part of the relationship between public and organizations.

One major aspect of this approach is the idea of 'dialogue' as a theoretical framework for extending public relations theory from symmetrical models to dialogic orientations. Botan (1997) suggested that dialogue manifests itself more as a stance or an orientation rather than a specific method, technique or format. In respect to traditional approaches, the dialogue elevates publics to the status of communication equal with organization and it provides a theoretical base for ethical public relations that challenges symmetrical models.

This is one of the last step made over the past 20 years towards the strengthening of PR theoretic ground in an attempt to repair some of the theoretic debts it owes to communication field. Even though we find out that public relations cannot yet hold its own in theory development with the older areas of communication, we can state that it has evolved into a major area of applied communication based in research of significant quantity and quality, becoming much more than just a corporate communication practice (Botan & Taylor, 2004).

MEASURING THE VALUE OF PR PROFESSION. SOME TECHNIQUES

Measuring relationship in public relations is an important task basically because both practitioners and scholars, in a growing number, have come to believe that the fundamental goal of PR is to build and then enhance on-going or long-term relationships with organization's key constituencies. Up until now, measuring the success of long-term relationships still remains the main problem, in part stem from public relations efforts (Hon & Grunig, 1999).

By using the word 'measurement', we consider a specific four-step process, as Joseph Raymond Roy defines (2009):

1. **Defining:** defining the results that your program intends to promote.
2. **Assessing:** assessing the dollar values of these potential results.
3. **Tracking:** tracking actual results and determining whether your program promoted them.
4. **Adjusting:** adjusting your program based on the tracking; doing more of what works well and less of what works not so well.

The main aim of this process is to make marketing and public relations programs more profitable by several repetitions until the programs reach up to the point where, for all practical purposes, they can't be optimized any further.

In 1997, The Institute for Public Relations issued a paper summarizing the state of knowledge in the measurement and evaluation of public relations (Lindenmann, 1997). The guidebook attempts to set minimum standards for measuring and evaluating the effectiveness of specific short-term PR programs, strategies, activities and tactics against pre-determined *outputs, out-takes* and *outcomes*. Those interested in measuring and evaluating the effectiveness of PR efforts aimed at enhancing the long-term *relationships* that exist between organization and its key constituents.

The progressive evolution of the public relations profession has led companies to increase their investment in the sector. The larger investment made, however, forces PR managers in terms to define the results obtained by the press office in economic and qualitative terms. In financial terms, it deals with to define Return on Investment

(ROI) or Return on Marketing Investment (ROMI), aiming to illustrate to management the outcomes of its contribution. ROI is not the only criterion; others include key performance indicators, benchmarking and balanced scorecards. The Return on Investment indicates a *ratio* between gain and cost, namely it is equals the gain from a program minus the cost of the program, divided by the cost of the program:

$$ROI = (gain - cost) / cost$$

In focusing on measurement and evaluation of the public relations ROI, there are some guiding principles or key factors to consider at the outset. A crucial point is to differentiate between measuring PR *outputs*, that are usually the immediate and surface results (e.g. the amount of press coverage received or exposure of a particular message), PR *out-takes*, which are usually more far-reaching and can have more impact (e.g. determining if those to whom the activity was directed *received, paid attention to, comprehended and retained* particular messages) and PR *outcomes*, which measure whether communications materials and messages have resulted in any opinion, attitude and/or behavior of the target audience (e.g. did the program or activity change opinion and attitude levels, and possibly behavior patterns?) (Lindenmann, 1997). This concept of media Inputs, Outputs and Outcomes was pioneered by Jim Macnamara (1992) through his Pyramid Model of PR Research.

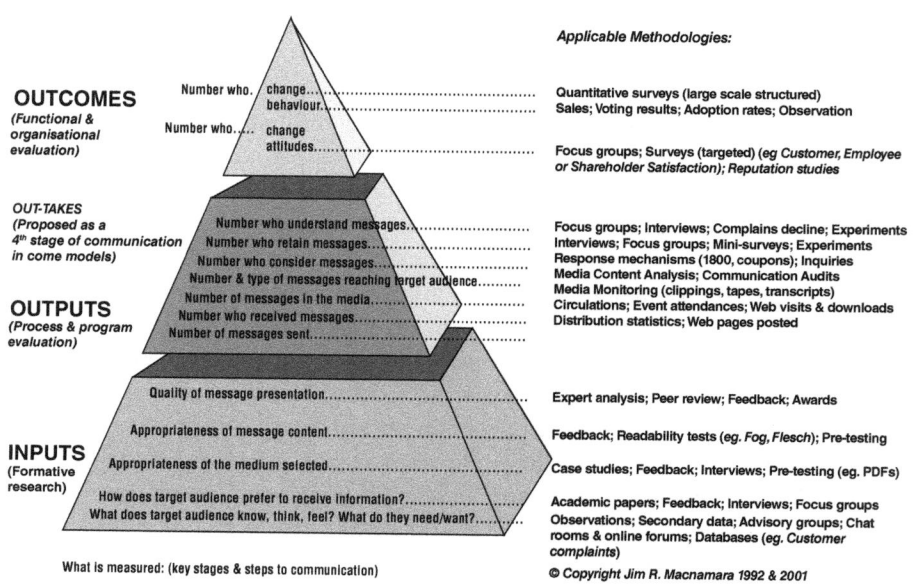

The Pyramid Model of PR Research is intended to be read from the bottom up: the base representing 'ground zero' of the strategic planning process, culminating in achievement of desired outcomes (attitudinal or behavioral). The pyramid metaphor is useful to convey that, when communication planning begins, practitioners have a large amount of information to assemble and a wide range of options in terms of media and activities. Selections and choices are made to direct certain messages at certain target audiences through certain media and, ultimately, achieve specific defined objectives (the peak of the program or project) (Macnamara, 2006).

The evolution of measurement activities can be divided into three stages at each of which the practitioners have begun a little better off than they had made in the previous stage by building on earlier efforts. Originally, practitioners used raw data to measure outputs of their activities, creating measures representing the output of a campaign, such as *column inches* and *impressions*. Now communications professionals are able to use knowledge about those *outputs* to measure the *effect* of their activities, for example to understand how the activities influence audience attitudes or consumer behavior (Argenti, 2005).

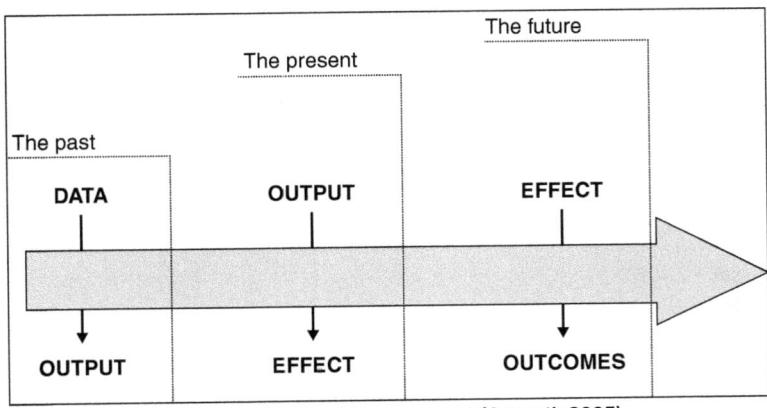

The Evolution of Communication Measurement (Argenti, 2005)

The communication industry must use information about the effect of its own activities to understand how they create value by contributing to companies' ability to meet their strategic objectives. Communication industry measurement produces data linked to a myriad of communication activities in order to understand the outcomes of its practices. The only industry's hindrance has been its inability to use existing data to establish a link to business outcomes.

In developing the capability of understanding the value that it creates, public relations sector has adopted the traditional measurements in order to analyze the media coverage that PR program has stimulated. These are *navigational* and *evaluative* metrics (Roy, 2009). The former help to navigate programs in the general direction of higher profitability, but they can't actually do anything toward measuring your profitability. The latter cannot, by themselves, measure profitability. However, they can help to steer programs toward higher profitability by adjusting the program so as to more effectively gain the prospect's awareness, engagement, understanding, belief and favor, which generally will result in higher ROI (Roy, 2009).

According to Roy (2009), there are four popular PR metrics, traditionally navigational: Clip Counting, Media Impressions, Accuracy of Coverage and Advertising Value Equivalency (AVE). Among them, the Advertising Value Equivalency is the one that has generated much debate in the public relations industry (Grunig, 1999; Macnamara, 2000, 2006, 2008; Peng Kee-Abu Hassan, 2006; Jeffries-Fox, 2003; Blowers 2006). This debate focuses on both the reliability and the validity of the method. We dedicate the whole next chapter to the analysis of the "AVE debate".

In addition to AVE, there are other meaningful methods able to measure the economic value of public relations. *Opportunities to See* (OTS) and *Cost Per Mille* (CPM) are two media measurement techniques used to estimate the ROI of media coverage. OTS is a measure adopted by advertisers to determine the position and to reach their products. It calculates the number of times someone is likely to see a marketing message. Unlike "impressions", which is a raw number of how many times a message was delivered to some channels, *Opportunity to See* attempts to define exactly how many of those impressions represented an actual possibility of a person to see/hear them. This figure is equivalent to hits or visits of Internet viewers and it denotes the breadth of penetration of a particular message (Peng Kee-Hassan, 2006).

In PR, it is widely known as news impression which describes the number of people who may have read a news story or an editorial message. To measure the cost effectiveness of reaching these audiences, the prerequisite is to identify the overall expenditure of a particular publicity program that had been implemented.

CPM, that is normally counted as cost-per- thousand, is derived by taking a said expenditure to multiply by a thousand and then divided by the total news impression or OTS. In mathematical terms, *Cost per Thousand* (CPM) is the cost to reach one thousand people or households via a given advertising outlet or medium. (M is the Roman numeral for 1,000).

$$CPM = cost / (target\ audience / 1{,}000)$$
or
$$CPM = cost \times 1{,}000 / target\ audience$$

Media planners calculate CPM to estimate the efficiency of a campaign and to compare the costs of various media. But in order to be reasonably accurate, the comparison must involve media that reach roughly the same audience. This is a fundamental navigational metric. It is a coarse measurement of the cost of approaching target audience. It is an easy way to compare the efficiency of different media: for example, television *versus* print (Roy, 2009). Nevertheless, by itself, it provides no analysis.

The *Measurement by Kilogram* is another technique mentioned for demonstrating purported results of public relations. It consists in collecting press clippings within the focus on quantitative measurement, with little attention paid to the quality of media coverage (Macnamara, 2008). Furthermore, press clippings present quantitative measurement of outputs only, not of out-takes or outcomes. Press clippings, tapes or transcripts indicate only the reporting occurred in the media. They do not indicate whether target audiences read, saw or heard the information and, if they did, whether it influenced their attitudes or behavior (Macnamara, 2008).

PUBLIC RELATIONS AND ADVERTISING: A DISCUSSED RELATIONSHIP. THE "AVE DEBATE"

One of the first and easiest ways of evaluating effectiveness in news publicity is to count the amount of media coverage gained. *Advertising Value Equivalent* or *Advertising Value Equivalency* (AVE) has become a common used method that alleged the value of public relations or, more specifically, editorial publicity (Macnamara, 2000). It is also known as *Equivalency Advertising Value* (EAV), *Advertising Cost Equivalents* (ACE) or *Advertising Space Equivalents* (ASE). This concept goes beyond counting news coverage and explains how much money they would cost if they were purchased as advertising. It is a measure of the economic value of the space and time covered by print or broadcast media, considering advertising rates (Peng Kee-Abu Hassan, 2006).

AVE is calculated, specifically, by multiplying column centimeters of editorial print media coverage and seconds of broadcast publicity by the respective media advertising rates. In most applications, the total amount of editorial coverage is "valued" as if it was advertising, irrespective of its content and "tone[1]" (Macnamara, 2000). A variant is to multiply the values obtained for a coefficient, determined arbitrarily, which should reflect the idea that messages delivered through public relations is more

---

1. How an article would leave a target audience reader feeling, typically defined as positive negative or neutral or measured on a Likert scale.

credible than advertising and thus of greater value (3 to 1; 1,5 to 1; 8 to 1 etc). Equivalents calculated using multipliers are sometimes referred to as "PR Value".

However, AVE has generated several debates and disputes in public relations and communication field, concerning the reliability and validity of its application. Jim Macnamara (2000; 2005; 2008) is a stern opponent of this quantification approach. Not only researchers, but also public relations institutional bodies like Public Relations Institute of Australia (PRIA), the UK Institute of Public Relations (IPR) and the Institute for Public Relations in the US have condemned the use of AVE for validity reasons.

In order to provide a critical valuation of the "AVE debate", it could be useful to make a comparison between the nature of advertising and editorial media content, as Macnamara suggests (2008):

ADVERTISING	EDITORIAL
Is identified as a paid for/sponsored message from the advertiser (eg. self promotion)	Appears as independent comment under the imprimatur of the editor or a professional writer
Appears separated from the news of the day and some people pay less attention to advertising than news or other programs	Appears as news (fact)
Content is never critical or inaccurate as it is written by the client	Many contain criticism and inaccuracies
Is placed in selected media strategically important to the client	May be in unimportant media including some not relevant to target audiences
Positioning is often controlled (eg. with loadings)	May be well-positioned or poorly positioned
Layout and design is client determined for impact, including use of headlines and logos	Is laid out by sub-editors. No control of headlines or photos. Rarely uses logos.
Macnamara, 2008	

Research comparing advertising and editorial news reported to the Summit of the International Association for Measurement in PR, organized by International Association for Measurement and Evaluation of Communication (AMEC) and the Institute of Public Relations (IPR) in Barcelona in 2006, confirmed the fallacy of claims made in the PR industry in relation to 'ad equivalency' or even greater value of publicity over advertising. Besides the importance of goal setting and measurement, the PR community asserted that "AVEs are not the Value of Public Relations". There was near-total agreement on this principle in Barcelona (92%), but the group was split on what other validated metrics to use in place of AVE. The legitimate intent of this statement is not to debate the validity of AVE (which simply measures the cost of media space) but to move beyond this measure.

On closer inspection, however, if, on the one hand, *The Barcelona Declaration* states that "AVE do not measure the *value* of public relations", on the other hand it remarks that "measuring outcomes is preferred to measuring media results" (second principle). This principle suggests that outcomes include shifts in awareness, comprehension, attitude and behavior related to purchase, donations, brand equity, corporate reputation, employee engagement, public policy investment decisions and other shifts regarding a company, NGO, government or entity as well as the audience's own beliefs and behaviors. Practices for measuring the effect on outcomes should be tailored to the business objectives of the activities. This means that quantitative measures such as benchmark and tracking surveys are often preferable (some researchers suggest that, in addition to being descriptive, PR research is dominated by a short-term quantitative tradition) and, where it is possible, they have to work together with qualitative analysis. Furthermore, as we will explain in the following pages, despite declarations against AVE, many PR professionals still keep utilize it.

Another problem is the existence of negative editorial contents, poorly positioned, ambiguous or favouring competitive brands: in this case, researchers agree there are not equal effects of advertising and can have, instead, a deleterious impact (Macnamara, 2000).

"Guidelines and Standards for Measuring and Evaluating PR Effectiveness", published by the Institute for Public Relations in the US, gave another critical opinion on "Ad equivalency":

> "Most reputable researchers contend that "advertising equivalency" computations are of questionable validity. In many cases, it may not even be possible to assign an advertising equivalency score to a given amount of editorial coverage (for example, many newspapers and/or magazines do not sell advertising space on their front pages or their front covers; thus, if an article were to appear in that space, it would be impossible to calculate an appropriate advertising equivalency cost, since advertising could never ever appear there)". (Lindenmann, 1997; 2003, p. 10).

An increasingly large slice of public relations field is considering the advertising as a different creature from editorial output although both are placed to fill up media contents. Therefore, they are not equal and they should not have any equivalency value to advertising rate for editorial products. According to Peng Kee and Abu Hassan (2006), differences between these two communication activities are mainly attributed to the control of the messages. Advertising is totally controlled by a company while editorial publicity rests in the hands of media organizations. Accordingly, news stories are independent comments by journalists, while advertisements are paid messages that appeared on media and they can be shaped exactly to the requirements of the advertisers.

To calculate AVE, indeed, is not a problem in itself. Its problems stem from what it is called and how it is used. Calling it an "advertising equivalency" strongly suggests that a news story of a particular size has an equal impact to an advertisement of the same size in that publication. There is reason to believe that there is no simple way for the relationship between news stories and advertising to be compared. For instance, there have been studies in the field of journalism showing that, over the past two decades, the credibility of the news media has been declining as an increasing number of entertainment components are introduced into news stories and newscasts (Jeffries-Fox, 2003). Moreover, as James L. Horton (2006) states, publicity metrics involve a process rather than space measurements because, unlike paid media in which one purchases column inches or time publicity, it requires persuasion of an independent journalist to write a story.

There are several ways to measure publicity value, but they largely ignore the process of persuasion and the credibility of a journalist's independent assessment. Publicity relies on credibility, whereas advertising, with an emphasis on media buying, finesses it. An independent journalist must find a story credible before considering it, and, while reporting the story, he must continue to find it believable (Horton, 2006).

Today, public relations practitioners must be able to demonstrate that their efforts are worth many times more than their cost, and AVE offers this measure for PR effectiveness: in this regard, they have to ensure that they are getting value for money for their public relations activities. In general practice, top management expects proper evaluation reports, which have to be the most substantial and scientific as possible. If the submission of proper media evaluation reports to the top management is without monetary figures, it may also be difficult for the PR practitioners to justify the benefits accrued from this activity (Peng Kee-Abu Hassan, 2006).

So, the AVE method is still a popular approach, especially among practitioners who are required to cope with the requirements of reporting on media situations, proving the worth of their activities. Quantification of value was attempted by evaluating the assessment in print media exposures only. All earned news coverage for that particular PR campaign were measured for the media type, space, position and their corresponding advertising rates. Then, monetary value was assigned to every single piece of PR news in the way disbursements were made for paid media The process of Quantifying PR Effectiveness (Peng Kee-Abu Hassan, 2006).

In advertising activities. The advertising rates for the period under study, together with the circulation and readership rates, were acquired from respective media organizations.

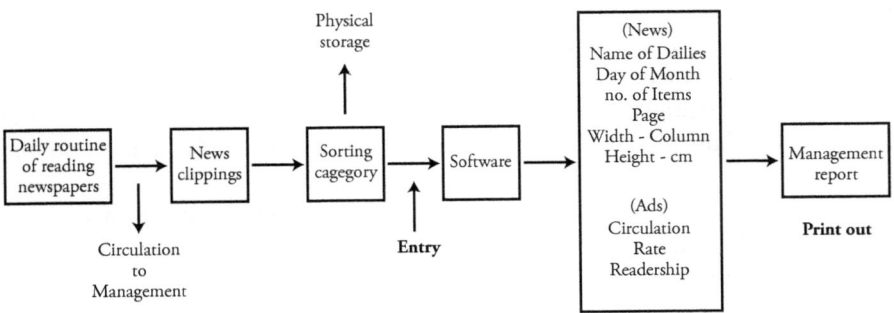

To solve management problem of summarizing the outputs of PR activities, practitioners use to adopt computer software able to quantify the economic value of news reporting. It is a quantitative mode of media treatment, which, to many researchers, is unsatisfactory in order to report the outcomes of communication programs.

The economic values in AVE measurement could then be worked out with the summation of news space multiplied by their corresponding advertising rates. (Peng Kee-Abu Hassan, 2006). This type of process is set up to understand how money has been spent efficiently. This attempt was in accord with the belief that PR activities ought to be measured against business activities and, then, how it impacted the business results. Besides that, it was also believed that this quantitative format of reporting could give an edge to the PR profession in business corporations that always demand facts and figures, as well as they wish to know the return on PR investments (Peng Kee-Abu Hassan, 2006).

Nonetheless, even though computer software are used to calculate AVE, this method has shown its limitations based on the assumption that advertising an PR use quite different methodologies. Valid comparison is therefore difficult. Some academics believe that the AVE method is able to describe ways of measuring the processes, instead of outcomes, of PR efforts in supporting business objectives (Peng Kee-Abu Hassan, 2006).

According to Tom Watson, Professor of Public Relations at The Media School at Bournemouth University and member of the Institute for Public Relation (IPR) Measurement Commission, in the first 50 to 60 years of public relations practice, research and measurement were largely ceded to market researchers or involved the collection of clips. It was not until the 70s that active discussion on measurement started at conferences and in academic and professional journals. It developed in the 80s and really exploded in the 90s, to become an enduring issue for research and discussion. This interest has led to regular measurement summits in the US, Europe and Middle East.

In Watson's opinion, the Advertising Value Equivalency is like a "pernicious weed", like a practice that has done more to undermine public relations than any other, still followed by most practitioners their day-to-day working life[2].

To sum up arguments for and against AVE, as Macnamara (2000) points out, we can gather those presented to support and to justify the practice in three points:

1. Correlations between volume of editorial coverage and outcomes such as change attitudes, share price rises and sales increase. In this case, it is important to distinguish *correlation* from *causation*, two entirely different concepts;
2. Both employers and clients ask for the use of AVE;
3. The market demand.

Arguments that show practical and ethical flaws in advertising-editorial equivalency are fundamentally gathered in eight factors (Macnamara, 2000):

1. Editorial publicity can be negative;
2. Editorial publicity can be neutral (advertising is never neutral);
3. Editorial articles often contains coverage of competitors including favorable references to or comparisons with competitors;
4. Editorial coverage can be poorly positioned;
5. Editorial coverage can be poorly presented;
6. Editorial coverage can be in non-target or low priority media;
7. AVE calculations are usually based on official advertising rates which are higher than the rates negotiated for advertising campaigns;
8. Advertising Value Equivalents only calculate the *cost* of buying equivalent media space and time for advertising; they involve no effort to measure the impact or effect of the content.

The last point is, perhaps, the most significant. It means that advertising and editorial publicity are rarely, if ever, equivalent, an assumption stemmed from a fundamentally different nature of the communications involved with news and advertising (Jeffries-fox, 2003).

In conclusion, we can state that the Advertising Value Equivalence, besides to be classified as a quantitative approach, becomes quite inadequate in reporting public relations outputs. The main conceptual limitations, as several researchers (Jeffres-fox, 2003; Macnamara, 2000, 2006, 2008, Peng Kee-Abu Hassan, 2006; Horton, 2006) indicate, is that the "Ad equivalency" only values what actually appears in the media, whereas it is often the case that public relation professionals counsel clients on behav-

---

[2] http://www.instituteforpr.org/2011/02/five-minutes-with%E2%80%A6dr-tom-watson/

ing in a way that purposefully results in an absence of publicity (Jeffress-Fox, 2003). So, as Peng Kee-Abu Hassan remarks (2006), we may have measured what PR has produced, but the ability to determine its success in generating wealth for a company remains unproven scientifically.

If we take a look to the PR practices, we discover that evaluation techniques require time and money. PR managers, indeed, have grasped the importance of measuring short-term results, with a reasonable budget. Currently, PR professionals have to find out proof of their work in order to succeed in today's competitive business environment. While other departments, such as sales, use hard numbers to demonstrate their impact to the business, to demonstrate public relations' outputs to the company has always presented a challenge for PR professionals. The overarching problem relies on less tangible and more time-consuming methods, such as clip counts and ad equivalency, to prove their value to the business.

Nevertheless, PR investments are integral to the success of today's leading companies. In a recent study to determine ROI of public relations, *Procter & Gamble* employed statistical modeling across the marketing mix of six brands over a three year period[3]. The study discovered that:

- Three of the six brands it studied showed public relations with the highest ROI of any marketing tactic;
- PR delivers significant ROI overall, much greater than advertising, and it provides a "halo effect" over other marketing tactics;
- PR showed an overall 275% ROI (the company used a statistical model called multivariate analysis that relates historical changes in which disciplines the company invested in to business results);
- PR delivers high ROI with relatively low spend in comparison to other marketing vehicles.

Hans Bender, the manager of external relations at Procter & Gamble, has inferred that a public relations campaign has a much higher rate of return on sales than traditional forms of advertising.

Even though the Second European Summit on Measurement suggests to companies and PR departments going beyond AVE in measuring PR results, it also remarks that the effect on business results can and should be measured where possible (*third*

---

3   http://docs.google.com/viewer?a=v&q=cache:59PQKoVzAjwJ:www.vocus.com/seovocuswp/seopressreleasewp.pdf+Overall+PR+delivered+a+275%25+ROI&hl=en&pid=bl&srcid=ADGEESg0JfmXx2Z306rUZXui6bQol44i4Mp4ntelIFD3DLUEsKgORAX4ppx2ZFaytHdgRF0lfX70EX94r7CxZIdQHayPY9KzpgSr0-9EqEFf9kYxHG_CzUGslcxVvhioZ1QotN8TFMnc&sig=AHIEtbT8mKiupEWpS7Dugmu15oazL6DSOg

principle). Thus, models that determine the effects of the quantity and quality of PR outputs on sales or other business metrics are a preferred choice.

Since public relations is a broad profession and may cover a wide variety of disciplines -media relations, online engagement, crisis communications, public affairs, executive counseling, brand building, events, reputation management, employee communications and financial communications to name a few- it is difficult to conceptualize the totality of the value that it delivers to the organization. Even though advertising equivalency modeling is not the answer to PR measurement, it is one of the solutions that PR managers use more often. For some companies with large marketing investments, diverse marketing tactics and visibility into end sales, it may be the best answer for demonstrating return on investment for public relations.

MediaMarket is an European media intelligence agency that provides media monitoring and consultancy[4]. In order to yield concise and powerful report that justifies PR activity, the agency realizes that the AVE measurement allows a company to assess its coverage, based on the volume of editorial secured being valued against the publication advertising rate card. In this sense, AVE still remains a basic measurement of media coverage. In this regard, the use of multipliers could be useful to recognize that positive editorial is worth more than advertising and neutral coverage is worth in any case.

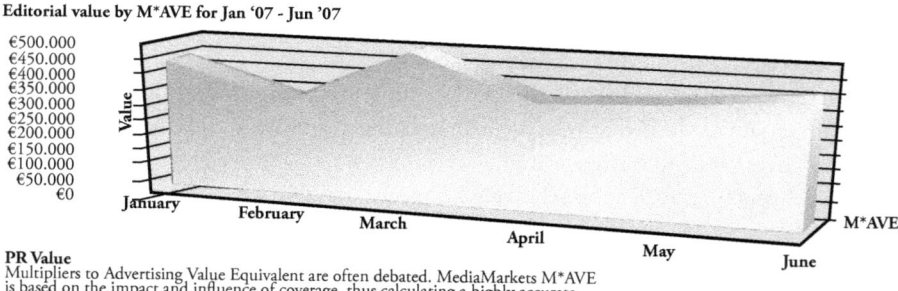

Multipliers to Advertising Value Equivalent are often debated. MediaMarkets M*AVE is based on the impact and influence of coverage, thus calculating a highly accurate value of what PR coverage is worth to an organisation.

As Chang Peng Kee (2006) points out, AVE could help to generate a systematic and objective way of analyzing PR campaigns for media evaluation research. In this way, monetary figures could provide some indicators of what have been achieved by the management. A systematic assessment of performance and results is an important step in PR evaluation. These efforts involve measuring the consequence of a program against the objectives that have been clearly set during management meetings.

---

4   http://www.mediamarket.ie/statyczna.php?menu_id=19

Public relations and advertising, moreover, share many similar characteristics in disseminating a company's information and they are treated as playing communicating roles within management functions. An advertising department has the responsibility for affecting the demand for the company's products by changing consumer taste and encouraging brand loyalty. On the other hand, corporate public relations serves to enhance company's image and reputation through news publicity. The efforts of PR practitioners are not worthless and should not be discarded when measuring the outputs of news publicity gained by the companies. In this frame, AVE, with all its flaws, seems to be the only method that has provided the possibility to quantify the economic value of PR news generated by the efforts of PR departments.

In 2003, the Commission on Public Relations Measurement and Evaluation states that "recent studies yield evidence that using the cost of media space and time provides a very useful evaluation of the news medium itself". Furthermore, the authors of the paper remark that, despite all the bad press associated with AVE, about half of all who measure their PR results still use it as of 2003. In 2009, a global survey on a sample of 520 PR professionals carried out by *Benchpoint* for AMEC, the International Association for the Measurement and Evaluation of Communication and the Institute for Public Relations, placed AVE in third place as most-often utilized measurement method, with press clippings and internal reviews being in positions one and two[5] with high level of satisfaction:

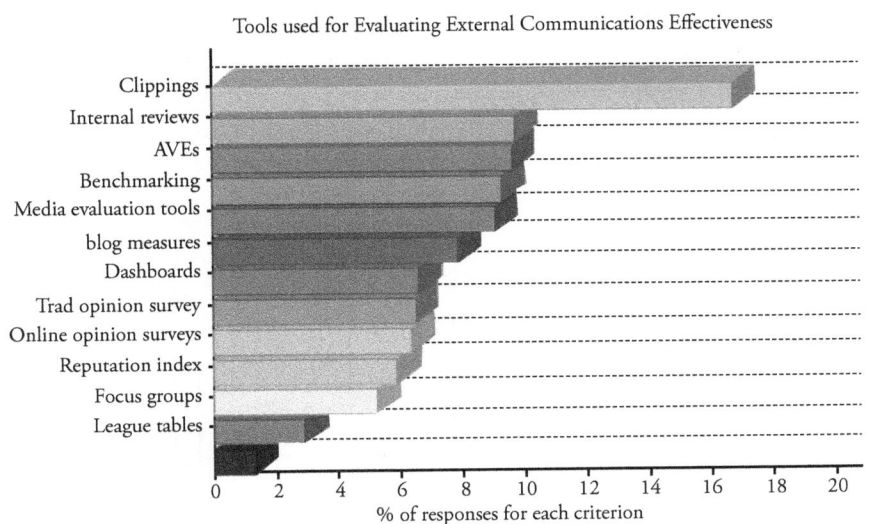

---

5 benchpoint.com/summit.pdf

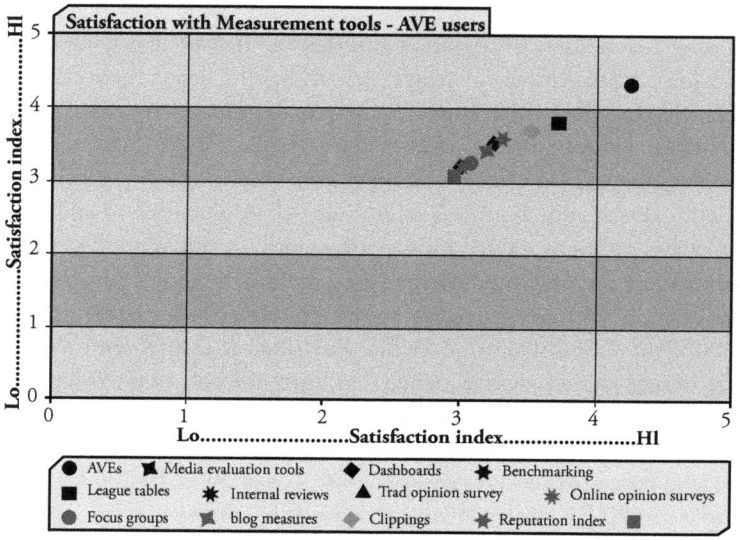

Moreover, if we consider an important variable such as company reputation, it is possible to discover that strong brands do not automatically have a strong reputation. In order to have a strong credibility, brand managers, included PR practitioners, have to built trust, respect and support in public perception.

Very recent studies carried out by the *Reputation Instititute* have supported this approach, remarking the strict tie between reputation and media exposure. Achieving coverage in the press, titles, articles etc, where target audience is most prominent, is critical, being that the media pool is ever increasing.

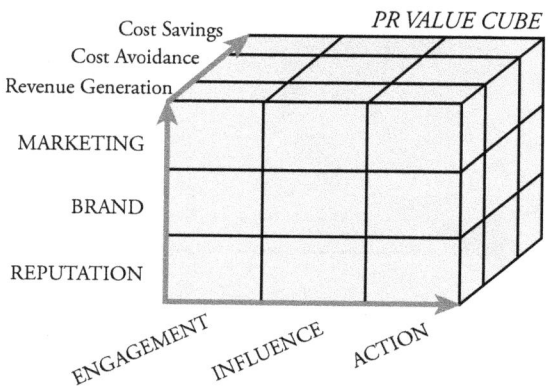

The PR Value Cube is a tops-down conceptual framework built for capturing all the ways PR gives value to the organization. PR contributes value in one of three major, interrelated areas (Y-axis). Building a good reputation is one of the primary overarching purposes of PR, usually measured more through the "gut metrics" than the analytical ones.

There is one more important consideration when we think about the total value delivered by public relations, which is time. PR creates value both on a transactional, short-term basis (e.g. the value of 10,000 potential customers reading an article in today's "X" newspaper) and on a process-oriented, longer-term basis. Brand and reputation are both examples of long-term values. So they are not immediately valued in terms of ROI, even so they are linked to media coverage and press exposure, which are measurable in quantitative terms trough AVE.

As *Reputation Instititute* tracks show, in order to build a strong reputation among customers, stakeholders, partners, employees and policy regulators, companies have to increase and improve their visibility in global and local market. To reach this goal, it is necessary to keep up with media exposure and visibility, even though the quality of message delivered is neutral. In this regard, the merit of AVE is that it is low-cost and it can quantify performance in simple monetary terms, that all the management team can understand.

To come back to the beginning of our analysis, it is useful to remark the difference between measurement and evaluation: if the former implies counting and quantitative short-term approach, the latter brings context and qualitative methodologies. Thus, if PR people take a systematic approach to define the values within their own organization, the risk of being "undervalued" will be greatly minimized (Porter, 2009).

EVALUATION BEYOND AVE: A QUALI-QUANTITATIVE PROPOSAL

The ability to evaluate the press coverage is a public relations practice that still affords a certain resistance among communication agencies and press offices. Public relation managers have always afford the problem of quantifying the actual PR worth in terms of Return On Investment (ROI). Big companies require more sophisticated methods in order to measure and to account set objectives, performances and competitive comparisons.

Even though many PR professionals still hold to the belief that public relations cannot be measured, partnerships between PR professionals and managers are increasingly common in order to create better methods to show a tangible ROI. Gather the clips for the month, detail the efforts in carefully worded prose, convey the strategy and plan behind the efforts are fundamental activities done on the ground of the most accurate calculations possible.

In this frame, Glebb & Metzger[6] and Raoul Romoli Venturi[7] work together in order to set up better and correct methods able to demonstrate a more complete picture of the impact of public relations and the type of measurable ROI that executives use to determine business objectives. The starting point of their work and reflection is the need to set more specific criteria in order to show the economic value of PR activities. Their efforts aim to underlie the quality of results over quantity.

In order to more accurately gauge PR success, organizations must measure the quality of their news not just the quantity. In order to do this, greater insight into news coverage is required. It is important that your analytical tools can measure more than just how many clips you have received. Glebb & Metzger and Romoli Venturi recognize that not all releases and articles are created equal, so why would the front page of a daily newspaper and a brief in an obscure press magazine with limited readership, each count the same? The prominence and the height of press coverage make all the difference.

Glebb & Metzger and Romoli Venturi, indeed, have striven to elaborate a more sophisticated measurement tools able to track where and how often news appear in an article. Furthermore, this method aims to score the impact of the press releases by assigning a weight based on the importance of the news; it also intends to give a positive, neutral or negative assessment of each criterion that makes up the company visibility. This keeping in mind that positive, negative and neutral scores are the results of a subjective evaluation that could be differently judged from different perspectives.

Starting from several recommendations provided by the second European summit on Measurement in PR, the Glebb Romoli Venturi (GRV) model comes from the need to implement qualitative approach into quantitative measures, such as benchmark, tracking surveys and, obviously, Ad equivalency. According to the authors, the added value of their own method is that it is not a comparison more or less optimistic between media coverage and advertising rates (like AVE), but rather it aims at finding out quali-quantitative features of press releases: space, visibility, prominence and readership. This kind of approach, indeed, attempts to balance two fundamental requirements: to satisfy financial *ratios* demanded from executives and to provide economic value of PR activities, which is reasonably related to the market.

---

6   http://www.glebb-metzger.it
7   Glebb & Metzger is a communication agency with offices in Turin and Milan. For several years, it has been involved in offering its customers PR assistance and systems for assessing the value of their work. Raoul Romoli Venturi is Communication and PR Director of Ferrero. He had been in the past in the Board of Directors of Martini & Rossi, being responsible for the communication area.

We can consider the GRV method as an evolution in qualitative terms of AVE. To better understand this new approach, we have to assume that an entire press release, a picture, a citation in the title have more influence in company visibility rather than an equivalent in size advertising message. Accordingly, it becomes necessary to produce suitable metrics able to consider all these kind of variables, in order to better evaluate company investments in communication campaigns.

The GRV method starts from the AVE calculation and goes beyond it, rectifying the equivalence "one to one" on the ground of the quali-quantitative features. Technically, the calculation aims to find out the Rectified Advertising Value or REAV. After calculating AVE considering the advertising rates, the amount obtained is multiplied for several coefficients referring to the media coverage obtained by the company and brand. This procedure reflects the idea that messages delivered through public relations are more credible than advertising and thus of greater value. It consists in scaling down the press items based on their features (if they are fully dedicated or included within the same discourse, or if they only contain a single citation unrelated to the company context).

Coefficients are calculated as follows:

- If the article is entirely dedicated to the company or focused on one of its brand, the coefficient will be '1' as that one of AVE;
- If the article is not entirely dedicated, but provides a brief description, informations, opinions or pictures related to company or brand, it will be about a collective article, whose coefficient is 0,2. Thus, in this case, rectified AVE will be 20% of advertising rates;
- If the article merely shows a citation about the company or brand, the coefficient will be 0,05. The REAV will correspond to the 5% of advertising rates.

In case the article presents multiple contents, the calculation will be as follows:

- If the item is completely dedicated to the company and it also mentions its other brands, in this case you will calculate a coefficient of value "1" which must be subtracted from the coefficients listed above of all other citations or collective items that will be assigned to individual categories . The coefficient of the initial dedicated item, however, must not fall below the value of the citation coefficient, that is 0,05;
- If the press item is ranked as "collective" but it contains citations about the other brands of the company, the other coefficients should be subtracted to the relative coefficient 0,2. The original collective coefficient, like said above , must not fall below the value of the citation coefficient, that is 0,05.

To sum up:
Multiplier focus "dedicated" = 1
Multiplier focus "collective" = 0,2 ➔ AVE x multiplier focus = correct AVE
Multiplier focus "citation" = 0,05

The correct AVE presents a maximum threshold that can not be exceeded. This threshold corresponds to the advertising rate of two pages belonging to the headline under evaluation. For example, an item dedicated made up of 8 pages on any newspaper or magazine or another one made up of 6 pages on the same headline will have the same AVE equal to the value of 2 advertising pages on the same headline. Thresholds, coefficients and multipliers are established in order to gain a more credible result. In fact, if we compare the results, we will notice that advertising rates are higher than negotiated prices through the GRV method.

The value of single multipliers will be summed up and then added up to a value base "1", which is the original value of the corrected AVE. This calculation will provide a new value, the REAV, which allows to measure and compare among them press releases.

The multipliers chosen will be applied to the follow press features:

- FIRST PAGE DEDICATED: if the front page is completely dedicated to the company or brand, the correct multiplier will be 3, which is the sum between 1 (base value) and 2 (the multiplier assigned). The final increasing value will be equal, indeed, to 200%.
- RECALL IN THE FRONT PAGE: if the front page presents a recall of the item related to the company/brand, the multiplier chosen to indicate the value of the item will be "2". The final increasing value will be equal to 100%.
- "SHOWCASE": it deals with the publication of pictures beside product description. It presents an high value because it is about a commercial advice of the journalist to the readers. The multiplier assigned will be, indeed, "2", that will increase the value of 100%;
- TITLE: the citation of the company's name in the title increases its visibility, so the multiplier assigned will be "1,5", that is the increasing value of 50%;
- PICTURES: one or more pictures in the press release are certainly relevant, so the increase of the AVE value calculated referring to the pictures wavers between 80 and 120%. A simple picture related to the company or brand included in the item has a coefficient of 0,8%; this coefficient, added to the base of "1", will give a multiplier equal to "1,8". Moreover, if the size of picture is equal or bigger than 1/4 of the page, it will be added a further "0,20" (in this case, the total multiplier is "2"). If the logo in the picture is completely clear, there will be a further increase

equal to 0,2. In case the picture has both features (> or = 1/4 of page or a clear logo), the coefficient is maximum, equal to "2,2".
- CITATIONS IN CASE OF SPONSORSHIP: in the case of sport sponsorship presented through pictures where athletes wear branding uniforms, the coefficient will be "0,5", added to multipliers already calculated.

At the end of qualitative evaluation, we will get the value of REAV, which is the result of multiplication between multipliers and the corrected AVE:

$$\text{corrected AVE} \times \Sigma \text{ qualitative multipliers} = \text{REAV}$$

Together with the calculation of REAV, the proposed method combines the value of readership, that is the number of readers of the magazine certified by national Audipress, in order to provide additional value and to realize the extent of public readers. In case of multiple content items, the readership value is divided by the number of brands quoted in the press item, in order to get a total value not skewed by the number of readers "hit" by single citations in the item. The calculation of REAV and Readership as seen has been implemented in a special designed computer software by EcoAnalysis, a division of Eco della Stampa, which is one of the key European operators in the media monitoring industry. This software is able to turn qualitative data into quantitative data, allowing to measure the effectiveness of press office's activities through reports produced *ad hoc* or periodically (monthly, quarterly or annually). Once got the REAV and READERSHIP of the press release under evaluation, it proceeds to a further overall assessment through the calculation of the Press Quality Impact Index (PQII). The goal of the PQII is to find out a value that takes into account the price of the magazine page (target luxury or fold), suitably mediated by the spread of the same. With the value of PQII, indeed, the GRV model aims to add a qualitative imprinting on quantitative measurement, going beyond the mere ad equivalency.

Technically, the Press Quality Impact Index (PQII) corresponds to the REAV multiplied by readership and then divided into 1.000.000: the final mark is calculated in GRV unit:

$$\text{(REAV X READERSHIP)} / 1.000.000 = \text{PQII (in GRV unit)}$$

The GRV is the value unit that allows to evaluate the quali-quantitative impact of press coverage. It is not an economic value, but rather a benchmark. It provides a qualitative evaluation of REAV related to the circulation of the press. The index should be read in its temporal evolution and in comparison with other brands or companies. In this sense, the goal of the PQII and GRV is to provide a benchmark comparable to that one of other products, brand along time.

The GRV is a unit of measurement that may not be easy to be understood if it is read in Σ company or Σ particularly famous brand. Depending on the needs, you can use as index the following units:
KGRV = thousand of GRV
MGRV = millions of GRV
GGRV = billions of GRV

The GRV model – an exemplification

Here, we will analyze the visibility of a hypothetical company, its products and sponsorship, compared to the previous years. The starting point is the number of items.

Fig. 1			
	ITEMS		
	Y-2	Y-1	Y
Corporate name	879	1.093	1.164
Product X	54	57	148
Product Y	44	25	16
Product Z	1239	1.343	1.274
Sponsorship	770	1.291	1.431
TOTAL COMPANY	2986	3809	4033

In the Fig. 2 we provide the evaluation in monetary terms of each component. The economic value, though it is a benchmark, it gives a reasonable size of the advertising investments that would be necessary in order to have the same space of visibility created by the news with other means.

Fig. 2	RECTIFIED EQUIVALENT ADVERTISING VALUE (€)				
	Y-2	Y-1	%	Y	%
Corporate name	1.214.380	3.047.062	150,9	3.688.313	21,1
Product X	112.424	350.258	211,6	859.538	145,4
Product Y	59.810	73.837	23,5	114.616	55,2
Product Z	1.888.084	1.793.139	-5	2.188.150	22,0
Sponsorship	1.806.235	3.391.862	87,8	2.765.797	-18,5
TOTAL COMPANY	5.080.933	8.656.158	70,4	9.616.414	11,1

Above, we can see that an increase in the number of items does not match automatically an increase in the result and vice versa. The change will be influenced by the type of the article (dedicated, collective, citation, multipliers), by the headline (luxury, local, tabloid), with list prices quite different. We take, as an example, the product "X" with 3 more items between the years Y-1 and Y-2, which provides a rectified equivalent advertising value more than double. This result comes from a better quality of press coverage: more items dedicated and more space, even if the number is almost the same.

We can state that, if this result is not isolated, but rather it is regular in different products, this is provided by media PR work. If we consider the line of sponsorship in the year Y-1 and Y, we observe a decrease of value in the year Y in comparison with an increase in the number of items. This could be depend on the importance of news both about teams and about activities in the year Y-1, able to produce more specific press releases, whereas in the year Y there were many citations, but less prominent news.

The duty of a good PR professional is working in order to create news when there is lack of them. For big companies, indeed, it becomes necessary to have a general view of media releases, even keeping under analysis each component of the items. The Fig. 3 provides the readership related to the item we analyzed:

Fig. 3	READERSHIP		
	Y-2	Y-1	Y
Corporate name	226.211.000	334.320.878	431.263.309
Product X	14.558.420	29.831.000	92.142.667
Product Y	16.403.000	5.973.000	12.114.500
Product Z	481.675.710	584.102.148	510.292.909
Sponsorship	1.069.500.500	1.576.171.547	1.366.201.309
TOTAL COMPANY	1.808.348.630	2.530.398.573	2.412.014.694

These data are misleading if we consider them overall, because a positive item in a famous periodical has less weight in terms of readership than a citation in the main national newspaper. However, it shows the circulation because the periodical has a good economic value, but it has a narrower target readership too. This explains the need to match readership and REAV and determine the PQII as it shows in Fig. 4:

Fig. 4					
	PQII in KGRV				
	Y-2	Y-1	%	Y	%
Corporate name	274.706	1.018.696	270,8	1.590.634	56,1
Product X	1.637	10.449	538,4	79.200	658,0
Product Y	981	441	-55,0	1.389	214,8
Product Z	909.444	1.047.376	15,2	1.116.597	6,6
Sponsorship	1.931.769	5.346.156	176,7	3.778.635	-29,3

This table represents the combination of Fig. 2 and Fig. 3 and it expresses the value of PQII. We can observe that the wavering of the qualitative index gives not only an economic data, but also the level of readership gained. We can also remember that the PQII is only a benchmark, in comparison with PQII of other products in the same period or the PQII of the same product observed through its temporal evolution. The Fig. 5 shows the PQII of our case, which is positive if we observed it through a lapse of time.

Fig. 5					
	PQII in GGRV				
	Y-2	Y-1	%	Y	%
Total Company PQII	9.2	21.9	138,4	23.2	5,9

This table could be explain that there has been a bigger investment in media PR practices in the period Y-1 compared to the period Y-2. We can infer it observing the amount of number of items (only 28%) whereas the increase of PQII in the same period is equal to 138,4%. Meanwhile, we observe the increase in qualitative terms.

Besides the comparison between investments and results achieved by the same product in different periods, this method also allows you to compare with competitor and with its level of visibility.

INDISCRETO IL CUOCO DELLA NAZIONALE DI CALCIO CHE HA SERVITO I LEADER

«Grandi sì, ma golosi di Nutella»

— L'AQUILA —

QUANTO di più italiano nel luogo più internazionale che ci sia in queste ore. Sul tavolo dei grandi per colazione the, caffè, pane e... Nutella. Ieri mattina, si è materializzato nella caserma di Coppito il signor "Nutella", per i non golosi Claudio Silvestri.

Puntuale alle otto e trenta, l'ormai mitico cuoco della nazionale di calcio ha portato ai leader riuniti nella giornata conclusiva del G8 il breakfast preferito nel nostro mese da chi ha più di sei mesi: barattoloni di cinque chili della crema alla gianduia più nota del mondo. Meno prezioso del libro con la copertina di marmo che Berlusconi ha regalato ai suoi ospiti, ma forse più apprezzato, oltre tutto offerto anche nella versione asporto monodose.

«Sarkozy è stato il primo ad affondare il cucchiaio», racconta Silvestri. Al suo fianco, il compagno di avventura Andrea Giovannini se la ride. Hony soit qui mal y pense: sia vituperato, chi pensa l'abbia fatto per colpa di Carla.

Trentaquattro anni, fiorentino di nascita e viola per scelta, il cuoco che ha colpito al palato il presidente francese ha mollato per un giorno Gattuso e Buffon per venire in trasferta al G8. Nel suo grembiule blu d'ordinanza sia sui campi di calcio sia sui set televisivi, confessa che eè più impegnativo occuparsi dei nostri calciatori piuttosto che dei Big del mondo».

Non avevamo dubbi...Però: vuoi mettere la soddisfazione di vedere il cuoco personale di Obama o i leader africani alle prese con la Nutella? L'unico a non tuffarsi pare sia stato Gheddafi: «Ha parlato dall'inizio alla fine del buffet». Tema del giorno, la fame. Chissà se il senso di colpa per aver goduto di tanta prelibatezza ha contribuito a rendere più generosi i grandi della Terra.

an. co.

Calculation of REAV and PQII on "Nutella". Examples

Example 1 : ITEM "DEDICATED"

QN – Giorno – Nazione – Resto del Carlino
July, 11th, 2009
<<Grandi sì, ma golosi di Nutella>>

Date of publication: 07-11-2009

Headline: QN – Giorno – Nazione – Resto del Carlino

Type of headline: national newspaper

Area of the page (standard): 88.218 mmq

AVE of the headline advertising page (currently rate): 70.560 €

Area of item within the page: 14.536 mmq

AVE of the area occupied by the item : 11.626 €

Topic: Nutella

Subtopic: Nutella G8

Focus: dedicated (the item is dedicated to the "Nutella breakfast" given to the G8 leaders)

Multiplier focus dedicated: 1

Corrected AVE (AVE related to the area occupied by the item X multiplier focus): 11.626 €

Base (coefficient which will be added to, if any, the qualitative multipliers): 1

Qualitative multipliers in: Title (<<*Grandi sì, ma golosi di Nutella*>>): 0,5

Tot. (base + title multiplier): 1,5

REAV (corrected AVE x Σ qualitative multipliers): 11.626 x 1,5 = 17.439 €

READERSHIP: 331.000 readers

PQII [(REAV x READERSHIP)/1.000.000] : [(17.439 x 331.000)/1.000.000] = 5,8 KGRV

Reasonable comparison with the 3:1 ratio method "press release vs advertising":
Method 3:1 = price list discount of 70% per applied multiplier ratio 3[8]:
70.560 − 70% (70.560) = 21.195 €
21.195 x 3 = 63.585 €
vs
REAV = 17.439 €

Example 2 : "COLLECTIVE ITEM"

Il Sole 24 Ore
May 31st 2010
<<*Il marketing in formato mondiale*>>

---

[8] The discount of 70% is generated by a prudential assessment. This discount is assigned in order to gain a very low negotiated price to which the multiplier 3 is applied. Accordingly, you will find out that the GRV Model brings about a more prudential REAV than the real value.

Il Sole 24 ORE

Calcio e business. Imprese in campo con iniziative specifiche per seguire gli azzurri in Sudafrica

Marketing in formato mondiale
Tra concorsi e merchandising un giro d'affari da 150 milioni

A CURA DI
Michela Finizio

Dentro i supermercati, nei negozi di elettronica e perfino alle poste è iniziato il count down. Le partite dei Mondiali stanno per iniziare, la prima è fissata per l'11 giugno, e dovunque ti giri nessuno perde l'occasione di promuovere o vendere qualcosa in nome del Sudafrica. Il marketing generato da un evento del genere in Italia frutta circa 30 milioni di euro solo di sponsorizzazioni ufficiali della Nazionale. Senza contare l'enorme business indotto tra premi, diritti tv, scommesse e iniziative collaterali: un pacchetto di investimenti, tutti pronti a sfruttare l'occasione, che arriva a sfiorare anche i 150 milioni di euro.

Gli sponsor

A sostenere gli Azzurri sono ben 27 marchi storici italiani che li accompagneranno in Sudafrica e terranno viva l'attenzione dei tifosi con centinaia di promozioni, gadget, concorsi e sondaggi. Per loro la partita più importante si gioca tra i consumatori ed è già iniziata da qualche mese. I contratti sono quadriennali o triennali e alcuni scadono proprio dopo il Mondiale, in tempo per partecipare alla sfida. Lo sponsor tecnico della Nazionale è sempre lo stesso, la tedesca Puma, che dal 2003 fornisce l'equipaggiamento necessario ai campioni del mondo (ad eccezione delle scarpe, che ogni calciatore può scegliere liberamente in base alla propria comodità). Negli ultimi trent'anni si sono avvicendati Adidas (1974-1978), Coq Sportif (1979-1984), Diadora (1985-1994), Nike (1995-1999) e per ultima Kappa (2000-2002).

La Puma, dopo il successo di Berlino 2006, ha rinnovato il contratto stanziando per il quadriennio 2007-2010 60 milioni (+15% rispetto ai quattro anni precedenti), circa 15 milioni all'anno. Lo sponsor tecnico scommette, inoltre, sui piazzamenti della squadra offre un premio importante in caso riesca ad arrivare di nuovo fino in fondo: per dare un'idea, agli Europei 2008, ad esempio, la vittoria valeva 3,3 milioni. A seguire ci sono gli altri brand ufficiali tra cui quelli storici (come Nutella e Uliveto) ed alcuni più recenti (come Actimel): il loro contributo per il quadriennio ammonta in totale a 56 milioni di euro (+30% rispetto al 2003-2006).

Marketing e merchandising

A far discutere nei giorni scorsi è stato lo spot della Peroni, che ha deciso di etichettare le sue bottigliette ambrate ricordando i risultati più importanti degli azzurri e su quella dedicata al 1938 compare il fascio del littorio: dai social network è partita la polemica e gli inviti al boicottaggio, ma l'azienda si difende dicendo di «aver scelto di riprodurre il più fedelmente possibile la storia della Nazionale».

Concorsi e raccolte

Le iniziative per i collezionisti abbondano: oltre alle etichette Peroni, è possibile raccogliere la *limited edition* di bicchieri Nutella o le calamite a forma di bottiglietta Actimel. E perché no, tentare la fortuna con le decine di concorsi a premi indetti per l'occasione, come quello della "squadra del bucato perfetto" della Omino Bianco per vincere maglie azzurre e palloni ufficiali. L'unico sponsor istituzionale, infine, è la Regione Calabria del 2008 (con 1,7 milioni di investimento per tre anni): dopo la campagna con Rino Gattuso per rinnovare l'immagine del territorio, durante le partite del Mondiale la Regione ha programmato una serie di spot radiofonici.

Il confronto internazionale

Il marketing italiano, dunque, arriva in ottima forma all'appuntamento dei Mondiali. Se questo dato sul campo avesse peso, gli Azzurri avrebbero tutte le carte in regola per ben figurare. Basta pesare le sponsorizzazioni degli avversari più temuti. La nazionale spagnola di calcio, dopo il trionfo negli europei del 2008, ha riscosso un grande appeal tra gli sponsor e quest'anno ha firmato 17 contratti che fruttano alla federazione 26,5 milioni di euro all'anno, di cui 3,5 garantiti dai primi cinque marchi: Iberdrola, Chevrolet, Adidas, Cruzcampo e il ministero per l'Industria il Turismo e il Commercio. Oltreoceano, invece, la nazionale brasiliana ha raccolto dieci sponsor, per un totale pari a 8 milioni di euro al mese: Nike è l'unica marca presente sulle magliette in campo e per il privilegio paga 35 milioni di euro all'anno; gli altri, tra cui Telefonica e Ambev, hanno budget inferiori.

© RIPRODUZIONE RISERVATA

Date of publication: 05-31-2010

Headline: Il Sole 24 Ore

Type of headline: national newspaper

Area of the page (standard): 141.828 mmq

AVE of the headline advertising page (currently rate): 257.485 €

Area of item within the page: 61.540 mmq

AVE of the area occupied by the item: 111.724 €

Topic: Nutella

Subtopic: Nutella

Focus: collective (the item provides a brief comment on an initiative by Nutella tied to the World Cup)
Multiplier focus dedicated: 0,2
Corrected AVE (AVE related to the area occupied by the item X multiplier focus): 111.724 x 0,2 = 22.345
Base (coefficient which will be added to, if any, the qualitative multipliers): 1
Qualitative multipliers in: None
Tot. (base + title multiplier): 1
REAV (corrected AVE x Σ qualitative multipliers): 22.345 x 1 = 22.345 €
READERSHIP: 1.122.000 readers
PQII [(REAV x READERSHIP)/1.000.000] : [(22.345 x 1.122.000)/1.000.000] = 25 KGRV

Reasonable comparison with the 3:1 ratio method "press release vs advertising":
Method 3:1 = price list discount of 70% per applied multiplier ratio 3:
257.485 − 70% (257.485) = 77.245 €
77.245 x 3 = 231.736 €
vs
REAV = 22.345 €

CONCLUSIONS

At the end of this dissertation, we resume some critical points handled. First of all, the emergence and development of critical work in the field of public relations. We have remarked the difficulty of defining theoretical frameworks for a management discipline that presents multiple perspectives of analysis. Some efforts have been made in order to reach a much broader understanding of public relations as a practice that has evolved to the status of a profession, which plays a major role in contemporary business world and society.

The main theoretical challenge met by both academic researchers and PR professionals concerns the debate about the use of qualitative and quantitative approach in measuring and evaluating PR results. Like other management disciplines, public relations has to be able to produce more benefits than costs as well as to point out tangible results quantifiable in monetary terms: business leaders are interested in investing capital in activities and assets for which they risk and return characteristics can be objectively measured, analyzed and predicted with some degree of certainty based on data and facts (Argenti, 2006).

In this regard, a number of attempts have been made to establish both quantitative approaches and qualitative metrics. Often, we tried to combine the different approaches as in the case of the Glebb and Romoli Venturi (GRV) methodology. With the calculation of REAV (Rectified Advertising Value), the GRV method aims to become an evolution in qualitative terms of AVE (Advertising Value Equivalency) and to better demonstrate, indeed, the Return On Investment (ROI) that executives use to determine budgets.

We have also reported the features of the dispute over the use of the Advertising Value Equivalency (AVE), which is one of the first and easiest ways of evaluating effectiveness in news publicity. AVE has generated several debates and disputes in public relations and communication field. There are two fundamental argument that support the disagreement on the AVE method: the existence of negative editorial contents and the fact that editorial outputs and advertising messages are not equal and they should not have any equivalency value to advertising rate for editorial products. Nevertheless, we take note of two arguments. The first one is that the advertising rate is highly flexible and the credibility of journalistic articles is normally higher than advertisements. Secondly, even if critics refuse to endorse AVE as a measurement tool, they cannot deny that there are situations and methodologies in which the advertising rates obtained can be useful. (Peng Kee-Hassan, 2006). Since these rates are an indication of relative credibility, using advertising rates as a factor in analyzing media value should not be a dispute.

Starting from the acknowledgement that there is no perfection in any single method or tool in measuring PR effectiveness, the Glebb Romoli Venturi model has striven to improve the simple AVE through the use of qualitative multipliers. With the establishment of indicators such as REAV and PQII, together with the use of some qualitative coefficients and readership index, the Glebb-Romoli Venturi method aims to build a valid benchmark able to provide a more reasonable measurement of press releases. Thus, this technical tools can become useful also to provide a better evaluation of the six dimensions that make up the "Harris-Fombrun Reputation Quotient"

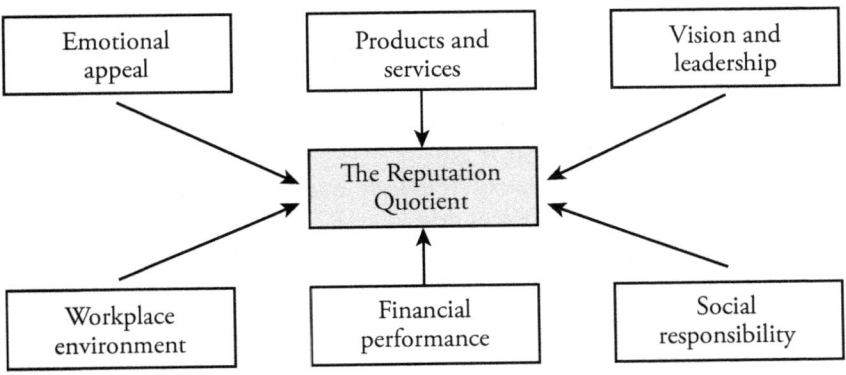

As Gary Davies (2003) remarks, 'reputation' is still a woolly concept, a mixture of constructs that appears to be evolving from what we still call 'public relations'. The role of what is now called 'corporate communications' or 'corporate affairs' is already broader than that of PR and one stage in the possible evolutions of PR into reputation management. How, if and why reputation is linked to the financial performance of an organization is a controversial area (Davies, 2003). Nevertheless, senior managers appear to be convinced that this is true: which CEO would admit that having a bad reputation in the market is something that can still mean excellent financial performance?

Finally, we can state that, although criticized, AVE is found to be more realistic in solving a long-lasting communication problem for PR practitioners. The Glebb Romoli Venturi method represents a reasonable evolution of the ad equivalency, aiming to link the quantitative approach with qualitative tools. A further step, we can forecast, could be to underline the growing importance of key message and favourability analysis.

REFERENCES

Argenti, P.A. (2005). Measuring the value of communications. In Marcia Watson DiStaso (Ed.), *Changing Roles and Functions in Public Relations,* University of Miami.

Blowers, M. (2006). Cracking content. A guide to measuring the media, present and future. www.meresearch.co.uk/MEresearch/index_files/.../VersionForWebsite.pdf.

Boudreaux, J. (2005). A quantitative assessment of public relations practitioners perceptions of their relationship with the organization they represent. University of South Florida. scholarcommons.usf.edu/cgi/viewcontent.cgi?article=3786&context=etd

Davies, G. with Chun, R., Vinhas da Silva, R., Roper, S. (2003). *Corporate reputation and competitiveness.* USA: Routledge.

Horton, J.L. (2002). *What does it cost? The value of PR services.* www.online-pr.com/Holding/Whatdoesitcost-article.pdf.

Horton, J.L. (2006). *What's it worth? Publicity metrics reconsidered.* www.online-pr.com/.../Publicity_Metrics_Reconsidered___REVISED.pdf.

Jeffrey, A., Jeffries-Fox, B., Rawlins, L.B. (2003). *A new paradigm for media analysis: weighted media cost. ublished by the Institute for Public Relations.* www.instituteforpr.org/topics/weighted-media-cost/

Lane, A.B. (2007). Empowering publics: the potential and challenge for public relations practitioners in creative approaches to two-way symmetric public relations. *Australian Journal of Communication* 34(1):pp. 71-86.

Macnamara, J. (2000). Advertising Values to measure PR: why they are invalid. www.pria.com.au/sitebuilder/resources/.../advaluestomeasureprpaper.pdf.

Macnamara, J. (2006). PR metrics. Research for planning & evaluation of PR & corporate communication. www.carmaapac.com/downloads/PR%20Metrics%202006.pdf.

Michaelson, D., Stacks, D.W., (2007). Exploring the comparative communications effectiveness of advertising and public relations: an experimental study of initial branding advantage. Published by the Institute for Public Relations. www.instituteforpr.org/downloads/9.

Pecchenino, M. (2004). *Le relazioni pubbliche.* Roma: Carocci.

Peng Kee, C., Abu Hassan, M. (2006). The Advertising-Value-Equivalent (AVE) method in qunatifying economic values of public relations activities: experience of a public-listed company Malaysia. *Kajian Malaysia,* Vol. XXIV, No. 1 & 2, 2006.

Roy Raymond, J. (2009). *Marketing metrics and ROI: how to set up a measurement system that can double your profitability.* www.marketing-metrics-made-simple.com/metrics-primer.html.

Vocus White Paper. Measuring the marketing ROI on public relations. How to improve PR success and demonstrate value to the business. www.vocus.com/codies/Marketing_ROI.pdf.

Weiner, M., Bartholomew, D. (2006). Dispelling the Myth of PR Multipliers and Other Inflationary Audience Measures. http://www.instituteforpr.org/topics/dispelling-myth-pr-multipliers/

WEBSITES

Glebb & Metzger agency. http://www.glebb-metzger.it

Politics in the Web 2.0. Between trust and credibility

Emiliana De Blasio

FROM CREDIBILITY TO REPUTATION

In 2009-2010, CMCS realized a research about credibility in the Italian news system. One of the section of that research was focused on the relationship between web 2.0 and political information; we adopted the conceptual distinction between *access, interaction* and *participation,* using a perspective close to that of Nico Carpentier (2007) and to our own earlier works (Sorice, 2007; De Blasio 2008) on this topic. That theoretical frame is based upon a tripartition concerning the form of audience involvement in social media: *access, interaction, participation*(AIP). Using the AIP model we built a "taxonomy" of civic engagement, even analyzing the relationship between credibility (as a relational concept) and trust (as a meaning effect deriving from the relations between media, political actors and the audiences).[1]

But one of the first problem, in 2010 and nowadays, is to define the audience's performances facing to the media and their power of influence.

Individual and social performances in a range of contexts are best made sense of in terms of what Anthony Giddens (1993) calls the *structuration of social practices*. Contemporary audiences are an example not only of the merger of creativity and reproduction but also of performativity and involvement as social practices. In all our work on media audiences we have noted that the traditional and rigid distinction between creativity and social reproduction seems to have definitively disappeared. Of course, this does not mean that there are no audiences; just that audiences are very different from some years ago. At the same time, this does not mean that the so-called active audiences are "always" composed of

---

1 Some parts of this chapter have been partially published in De Blasio 2010 and De Blasio, Sorice 2010.

active participants. In the field of Web 2.0 studies, we have to consider the different ways in which one can approach and "live" social networks. Not always a participatory style. Networked individualism (Castells, 2001) is replacing the use of other types of social formations, such as – according to Virginia Nightingale (2007) – informal formations. This is a very important point when we try to study how the media can play the role of social influencer or that of definer of social reality.

FROM MISTRUST TO DISINTERMEDIATION PROCESSES: NEW STYLE OF PARTICIPATION

For this research, we have been working in the frame of a methodological approach which is close to *discursive realism*, while the theoretical basis is rooted in Giddens' *theory of structuration*.

The research, even if it is interdisciplinary and uses a holistic approach, presents some critical points; we have no definite answers, due to the complexity of social action produced by actors operating with knowledge and understanding as part of their consciousness. Our knowledge of the social actors feeds into their reasonable behavior (Giddens, 1984). And in this road there is the part of our research which is focused on the interrelationships between political engagement and social participation. Our theoretical starting point is that reflexivity plays an important role in the social and political practices activated in/through social networking. *"The reflexivity of social life* – as Giddens has stated – *consists in the fact that social practices are constantly examined and reformed in the light of incoming information about those practices, thus constitutively altering their character"* (Giddens, 1990: 28). In this frame, in 2010 we used both virtual ethnography methods and traditional focus groups (with people experiencing political communication in social networking). Similar research we have designed and realized in the second semester of 2011.

In both cases, we have avoided the study of the relations between contents and individuals, preferring a detailed investigation of the general landscape of people's media consumptions from the point of view of involvement and participation/activism. The aim of our 2010 study was to determine the interrelationships between social networking styles and political participation (including, of course, voting, attention to Italian social and political life, promoting and signing petitions, etc.). In this case we have preferred to focus our attention to how credibility in the media sphere and trust in the connection can constitute an important element to promote social legitimation and to improve the reputation.

Studying the civic behavior in the web 2.0, we have observed four tendencies:

1. The **growth of** networked individualism: in this frame we can locate some examples of social networking;
2. The **growth of involvement with an impact on civic attention and engagement**;
3. The **growth of new subjects (traditionally distant from the political sphere) approaching politics and pre-political forms of engagement;**
4. The fourth tendency (a direct consequence of the third) is the **growth of networking** as a tool **to increase social participation** but mainly in *subjects who already have political and social interests.*

Exploring the prismatic universe of the Web 2.0 spaces for Italian politics we can confirm a simple taxonomy concerning the main functions of websites, networks, blogs, etc. It is based upon four functions:

1. *Information*
2. *Fund raising*
3. *Involvement*
4. *Mobilization*

The fourth function —mobilization – is made up of three different levels:

a) *Representation* (concerning self-presentation and identity);
b) *Belonging* (it means to consider the political mobilization as community belonging)[2];
c) *Action* (that is the conscious civic engagement).

Crossing the three elements of the AIP model with the four steps of the political engagement in the web 2.0, we can trace a simple but useful schema concerning the different areas of the political participation.

---

[2] It can be useful to remind that, using this perspective, we predicted the rising importance of some web-based movements, such as the "Popolo Viola" or the Beppe Grillo's Meet-Up in the borning step of the "Movimento 5 Stelle" (Five Stars Movement).

Fig. 1. Communication Styles and Social Functions of Social Networks				
	INFORMATION	FUNDRAISING	INVOLVEMENT	ACTION
ACCESS	Social curiosity	Symbolic involvement		
INTERACTION	Information exchanges	Representational belonging	Civic Attention	
PARTICIPATION	Information Producing	Social engagement	Community (group) belonging	Political Participation

The definitions used for the taxonomy resulting from the table are a simplified representation of more complex phenomena. In the last ten years, participation has suffered some irreversible changes and, as Pippa Norris has emphasized(2007), these might be summarized as follows:

a) A general disenchantment with political parties by the electorate, manifested by a clear anti-party – and anti-political – sentiment (De Blasio, Hibberd, Higgins, Sorice, 2012) and a decline in membership in these organizations;
b) A more general decline in the significance of the traditional agencies of political participation in favour of new ones, characterized by more fluid boundaries, in the double sense of allowing easier entry and exit from the group and an extension that goes beyond national borders. These new agencies have a structure that aims to involve members in social changes and not only in traditional politics through social actions such as boycott actions and new lifestyle promotion;
c) The rise of cause-oriented activism, characterized by goals related to a single aspect of social life: consider also – in different way –the partial success of the "causes application" on Facebook.

The table in Fig.1 shows the presence of at least nine different "models" of social networks used for political communication. It is possible to draw a map derived from cognitive-behavioural responses to interviews and verbalizations of the participants in the focus groups we conducted in 2010 and in 2011. From the map – obviously the findings of a software-based method, not immune to criticism and therefore to be interpreted merely as a business tool– one finds two main styles which can easily be generalized and a border area of specific behaviors. The first style is that of the subjects who – with different nuances– show interest and knowledge of the social and political sphere (the "engaged"),whereas the second behavioral style is adopted by the people who instead manifest a certain skepticism about the horizontal nature of the relationship between citizens and politics in Facebook (the "lukewarm"), even if they consider positively the experiences of so-called Web 2.0. These subjects show a strong absence of *trust* on political topics("all politicians are just opportunists") and their use of social media seems to be limited to win the electorate's confidence.

To these two macro-trends we can add a large border area, represented by those entities that use the political potential of the network, but at the same time consider it exhausted in the network. The two (plus one) tendencies can be superimposed on the findings emerging from Table. The result is shown in the table in Fig.2.

Fig. 2. Communication styles and social functions of the social networks. People and behavioural logics.				
	INFORMATION	FUNDRAISING	INVOLVEMENT	ACTION
ACCESS	Social curiosity	Symbolic involvement		
INTERACTION	Information exchanges	Representational belonging	Civic Attention	
PARTICIPATION	Information Producing	Social engagement	Community (group) belonging	Political Participation
Legend: grey = *lukewarm*; medium grey = *border area*; light grey = *engaged/involved*.				

The "engaged" seem not to adopt "front stage" behaviors (typical of traditional political mediation) replaced by disintermediation practices; the lukewarm people seem more inclined to consider Facebook a simple evolution of political mediation. In reality, looking at the findings in depth we can observec ontradictory phenomena even among those people who most frequently use social networks as a place of knowledge, consensus and call for political action. In particular, the majority of our respondents both in 2010 and in 2011 do not underline the presence of real mechanisms of disintermediation, but a transformation of political mediation from vertical to horizontal and dialogic communication. It was difficult in 2010 and even more now to say whether our findings are also the result of the transformation (and sometimes dissolution) of the "party-form" or whether they are only a "meaning-effect" deriving from the relational characteristics of the social networks (Facebook particularly).

In "civic attention" and in "community belonging" we find many of the new experiences of political participation in Italy, from opposition to the racism and xenophobic to the many forms of antagonistic engagement (sometimes even in an anti-political position). Butt he se forms rarely become social commitment beyond the Internet, and there is therefore a risk of maintaining the gap between the imagined nation and the real one. In other words, the disintermediation processes don't seem to transform themselves quickly into new kinds of political intermediation. At least not always. At the same time audiences – even if surely no longer passive – seem only partially "participants".

TRUST AND REPUTATION

We have already proposed to study the relationships between trust and participation. Starting from two axes (trust-mistrust and access-participation) we obtained the following findings (as described in Fig. 3):

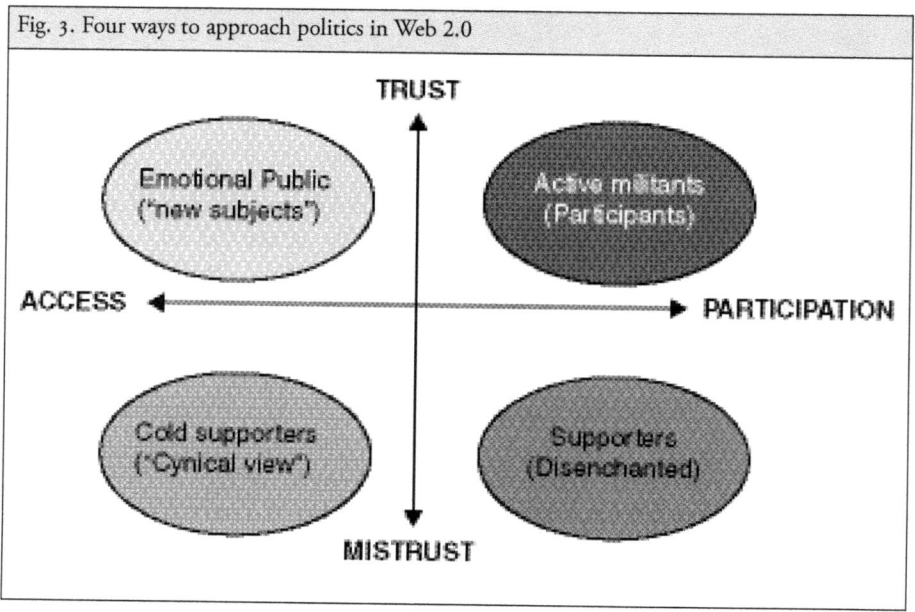

Fig. 3. Four ways to approach politics in Web 2.0

The social media seem to improved is intermediation processes in the relations between citizens and political actors. At the same time, this trend is not always evident and in some cases a new form of re-intermediation replaces the old one. The dynamics of trust seem to play an important role in the mechanisms of legitimation of political actors. In other words, if the new subjects of politics develop trust mechanisms within the same logic of "connectedness", people more traditionally sensitive to politics (such as the cynics) feel the need for new mechanisms of intermediation: non-traditional ones, not exercised by traditional political parties, buts till present and active.

Thanks to these considerations we can argue that - contrary to what many say – the social networks are not merely containers of political issues but are, at the same time, *frame, content and tool of legitimization*.
In particular, the majority of our focus group respondents highlight not so much the presence of disintermediation processes, but a transformation of political mediation into horizontal and "dialogical" communication styles.

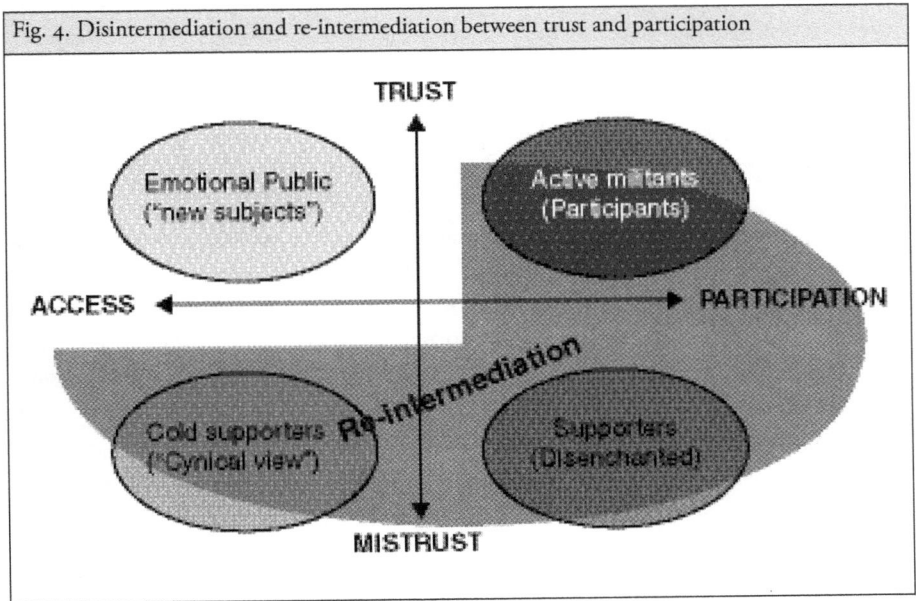

Fig. 4. Disintermediation and re-intermediation between trust and participation

SOME EXAMPLES

In some areas of political information (for example the local information, that is very often closer to the people's experience) the social media appear to generate greater credibility, in some cases even greater than that produced by the local press. The "para-participatory"dimension of the web, in other words, works as a control, authentication mechanism of sources: this process is not too dissimilar (beyond the production routines of course) than that of the citizen journalism. We can say that in these cases the credibility is strongly connected to the web as a social system (or, as in the case of citizen journalism, from the "history of credibility" that the website has gained towards its users).

The many researches on these topics have put in evidence how the web 2.0 can represent a source or even a multiplier to generate mistrust and lacking in reputation but also a space in which it is possible to improve social legitimation. An important analytical tool, in this context, is represented by the so-called *buzz monitoring*. It is an analysis concerning the users' comments in the several threads in which a political topic can be discussed. The buzz analysis – even if it is not comprehensive and definitive – can help the researcher to build conceptual maps or list of digitalizing argumentations and to analyze the weakness and the strenghtness of the delegitimisation process. It is possible to find the "buzz" in Youtube, in Facebook and in many other social media and, still, in the blogs' comments and answers.

In the course of the last two years we have studied many cases. One of the most interesting was represented by the so-called "Boffo case" (from the name of the former director of *Avvenire*, the catholic bishops conference's newspaper, falsely accused by another newspaper, *Il Giornale*, owned by Berlsuconi family, through a false police report).

Using the buzz monitoring (with the support of some specific software for social sciences), it is possible to draw figures such as the following.

The figure 5 shows a simple example of the frequency of keywords related to the comments on the credibility of the "Il Giornale" news concerning the "Boffo case". Note that the tag cloud of figure 5 concerns the "buzz" recorded on the days when the case was almost solved and it appeared clear the manipulative strategy operated by the newspaper, then admitted even by its director[3].

The tag clouds deriving from the buzz monitoring are not timely and precise tools, able to define a phenomenon in a unique way; they, on the opposite, show trends of the semantic aggregation of the people participating in the web. This analysis, jointly with consolidated methodology of social and political research, can help the researchers to enlight the way in which media can improve legitimisation or lower

---

3   For further examples, see De Blasio 2010.

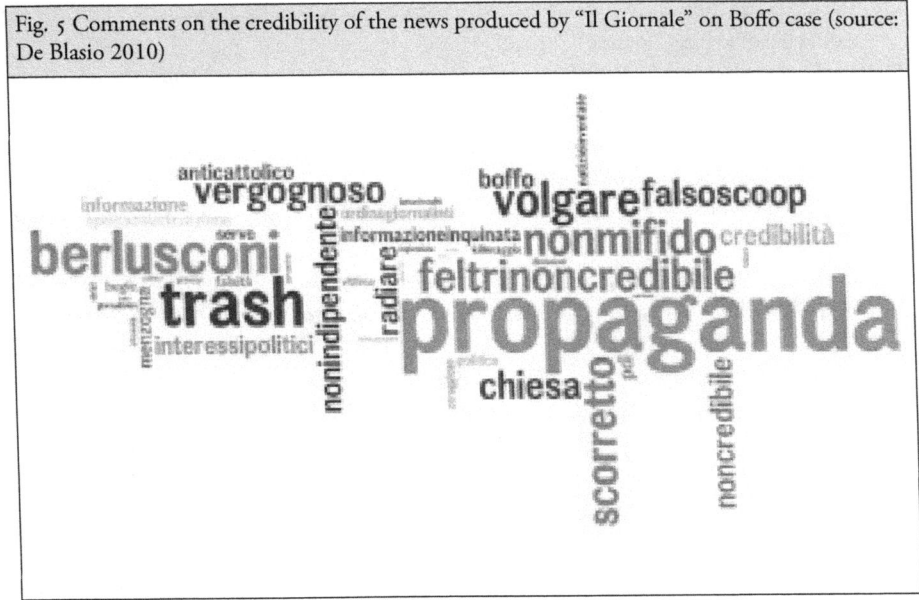

Fig. 5 Comments on the credibility of the news produced by "Il Giornale" on Boffo case (source: De Blasio 2010)

the reputation level. As, for example, in the so-called "mud machine" (macchina del fango) properly described in the next chapter. But, in the same time, these analytical tools can be also helpful for the public relations teams (or the spin doctors in the case of a politician) to effectively counter attack the discredit attempts.

REFERENCES

Cammaerts, B., Carpentier, N. (eds.) (2007) *Reclaiming the Media. Communication Rights and Democratic Media Roles,* Bristol: Intellect Books – ECREA.

Carpentier, N. (2007) *Participation, Access and Interaction: Changing Perspectives,* in Nightingale, Dwyer 2007.

De Blasio, E. (2009) "Il marketing politico" in Viganò, D. E., ed (2009) *Dizionario della comunicazione.* Roma: Carocci.

De Blasio, E. (2010) "Informazione e social media. Fra credibilità, fiducia e nuove intermediazioni", in Scandaletti, P., Sorice, M. eds. (2010) *Yes, credibility. La precaria credibilità del sistema dei media.* Roma: UCSI Unisob CDG.

De Blasio, E., Gili, G., Hibberd, M. Sorice, M. (2007) *La ricerca sull'audience.* Milano: Hoepli.

De Blasio, E., Hibberd, M., Higgins, M., Sorice, M. (2012) *La leadership politica fra media e populismo*. Roma: Carocci.
De Blasio, E., Sorice, M. (2008) *Involvement and/or Participation. Mobility and Social Networking between Identity Self-Construction and Political Impact*, in "Media, Communication and Humanity, Medi@lse Fifth Anniversary Conference. London: London School of Economics.
Giddens, A. (1984)) *The Constitution of Society. Outline of the Theory of Structuration*. Cambridge: Polity Press.
Giddens, A. (1990) *The Consequences of Modernity*. London: Polity Press.
Giddens, A. (1991) *Modernity and Self-Identity. Self and Society in the Late Modern Age*. Cambridge: Polity.
Giddens, A. (1995) *Politics, Sociology and Social Theory: Encounters with Classical and Contemporary Social Thought*. Cambridge: Polity Press.
Higgins, M. (2008) *Media and Their Publics*. Maidenhead: Open University Press.
Mc Nair, B. (2007) *An Introduction to Political Communication*. London: Routledge.
McNair, B., Hibberd, M., Schlesinger, P. (2003) *Mediated Access*. Luton: Luton University Press.
Nightingale, V., Dwyer, T., eds., (2007) *New Media Worlds. Challenges for Convergence*. Oxford: New York.
Rockeby, D. (1995) Transforming Mirrors: Subjectivity and Control in Interactive Media, in Penny, S. (ed) *Critical Issue in Electronic Media*. New York: State University of New York Press.
Servaes, J. (1999) *Communication for Development: One World, Multiple Cultures*. Hampton, New Jersey: Cresskil.
Sorice, M. (2009) "Comunicazione e Politica" in Viganò, D. E., ed. (2009) *Dizionario della comunicazione*. Roma: Carocci.
Sorice, M. (2011) *La comunicazione politica*. Roma: Carocci.

What is the macchina del fango: genesis and development of a political use of media power.

Noemi Trino

"La macchina del fango" (literally "the mud-slinging machine") is an Italian metaphor used by journalism to describe the coordinated action of a pressure group, in order to delegitimize and undermine the credibility or the "honour" of a person recognized as a dangerous "enemy" to be intimidated, punished or influenced.

The victim of this delegitimising machine is usually part of the complex structure of our democracy, since in our country, as Hallin and Mancini noticed (2004), "the newspapers, and later electronic media, actively participate in the struggles between the various ideological camps. "

The birth of this phenomenon is traced back by Giuseppe d'Avanzo, a political reporter for the left-wing newspaper *La Repubblica*.

How the machine exactly works is a controversial issue, involving a number of actors including journalists, professed political advisors and politicians, whose role is linked to the democratic degree of our political system.

The machine operates by collecting, often illegally, a number of sensitive and confidential information, hints and news, variously extracted, manipulated or even wholly false, concerning the life and work of the enemy to hit. These dossiers are spread (or simply vented) in order to exercise an indirect but strong public pressure on the activity or the personal freedom of expression of victims.

The central role of the media in creating and modulating crises is by no means new. There is much debate about the relative power of media and government elites in the crisis communication process. An extreme image portrays the media as lion more than a lamb, emphasizing their power in shaping public opinion. It "emphasizes the predatory and nihilistic nature of modern journalism, which casts the politician or bureaucrat in the role of prey. Some analysts speak of "attack journalism" where "packs" of reporters stray around as "junk- yard dogs" (as opposed to the more benign "watchdogs") looking for consumable dirt on political leaders and other actors inside and outside government". (Boin et al., 2005, p.74).

This method, which includes extrapolations, manipulations, falsifications of news with a clear blackmailer or defamatory purpose, finds its means of expression in the so-called Junkyard journalism.

Junkyard journalism marries aspects of muckraking to adversaries watchdogism. As Sabato said, this genre of attack journalism produces "political reporting that is often harsh, aggressive, and intrusive, where feeding frenzies flourish, and gossip reaches print. Every aspect of private life potentially becomes fair game for scrutiny as a new, almost "anything goes" philosophy takes hold" (1991, 26).

Junkyard journalism's model is useful in order to explain one, important, variable of the phenomenon, the one related to the role of journalism in our political system.

Examining the private lives of public officials, government ministers or candidates, to find some kind of less than exemplary behavior in terms of personal conduct, is often dressed up in the guise of public interests, and, increasingly, investigation into serious or potentially serious transgressions takes places in a news environment that is closed with exposés of questionable merit (Stanyer, 2007, p.111).

Private sexual misdemeanours are treated in the same ways as acts of dishonesty and financial malpractice in public life (*ibidem*).

It is true that we can consider the so-called "erosion of privacy" as a peculiar tendency of contemporary political communication The "mud-slinging machine" can be only partially ascribed to this model. On one hand, in fact, the politicians' visibility in a media-stuffed environment can be considered as a key feature of contemporary political communication system, even in our country. On the other hand, this flow of information from personal back region to the media, in Italy, shows how media are considered political actors which plays on their audience's fears in order to delegitimate a political enemy. Political news becomes, in this way, "backstage manoeuvres of campaign operatives to guide or influence journalists" (Esser et al. 2001).

This is not the only effect of such a system of (dis)information: as many authors underlined, the subversive power underlying the functioning of the mud machine seems to be even more devastating since it achieves its goal simply extending its menacing shadow over potential objectives.

A real "manufacture of consent" (Lippmann, 1954), whose rise represents a danger for the integrity of the public sphere. As Brian Mc Nair notices, "to the extent that citizens are subject to manipulation, rather than exposed to information, democracy loses its authenticity and becomes something more sinister" (Mc Nair, 2010, p. 24).

The evolution of the so-called "macchina del fango" puts its roots on the fundamental distinction between "persuasion" and "manipulation". As Mc Nair argues manipulation of opinion and concealment of inconvenient information are strategies emanating from political actors themselves, pursued through media institutions. In

Italy, the media have always been a part to the politicians' effort to conceal sensitive information giving to the public an incomplete and partial picture of reality.

THE AGENDA SETTERS: POLITICAL PARALLELISM AND THE ITALIAN PRESS

In order to understand the role and the success of such a (dis)information machine we have to introduce some fundamental features of Italian political system, starting from the assumption that, in contemporary democracies, media institutions perform not only cognitive functions of information but also interpretative function of analysis, assessment and comment (Mc Nair).

The gradual citizens' disaffection to political life and the consequent decrease in social participation are accompanied by new kinds of relationships between parties and citizens, which deeply influence the mechanisms of consensus-building.

The most common tendency is that of permanent campaigning. This concept, used for the first time in 1976 by Pat Cadell, an adviser to U.S. President Jimmy Carter, refers to the inherent tendencies of advanced societies in which the communicative dynamics of election campaigns are not limited to the times of ordinary political life, but tend to overcome them. As Michele Sorice wrote, "election campaigns' aim is no longer just to mobilise consensus around one candidate or party, but to reach that increasingly large swath of the uncertain and / or free-floating electorate"(2009).

This has led to important consequences: as Mauro Calise wrote, "the organisational and ideological collegiate system, by which the parties were active in the First Republic has been dismantled and replaced with a personal device. The parties are becoming machines to personal service of this or that political leader (2007, p.15) ".

For this reason, we have to start, as Mazzoleni wrote, from what is "a fundamental feature of political communication, that is its connection with the context and the rules of democracy: the exchange of symbolic resources for the conquest of power, to use Lasswell's words, the dialectic between the parties is possible only in a context of freedom and not coercion" (2004, 16).

The adoption of an approach based on what Blumer and Gurevitch called "hermeneutic of interaction media-politics", enables the investigation of the effects of the process of media coverage in different political systems.

In the Italian political system, one of the most common practice is the use of media as means to intervene in the political world. The radical nature of the ideological divisions and bitterness of the conflict made it difficult for the mass media system distancing from politics, also because of a historical lack of professional culture and organisation of the profession independent of policy options.

This had lead to a public sphere structured differently than in the other liberal countries; here, the main reason is the attempt of political communication actors to reach the mass audience of private citizens. Here, however, the heart of political communication is the process of negotiation that takes place between parties, factions and social actors in their allies. The outcome of this negotiation process is not based on shared rules because of a political culture much more inclined to partisanery, which facilitates the affirmation of patronage practices.

In other words, in Italy journals have always been viewed as part of hegemonic power game (Louw, 2010, 190). The media become embroiled in struggles over policy and meaning been fought out between various factions of the governing élite. Sometimes this may produce a "two-step effect"- i.e. try to influence the "general" public mood or the mood of specific interest groups, in the hope this will have an impact upon policy makers.

Il Giornale

The leading actor of the mud-slinging machine is the newspaper *Il Giornale*. Founded in 1974 by Indro Montanelli, one of the founding fathers of Italian modern journalism, *Il Giornale* belongs to the Berlusconi's family since 1979. It's the eighth most popular newspaper of the country: with a daily circulation of about 183.000 copies, it's the most read right-wing Italian newspaper.

The editorial direction of the newspaper has never hidden the open support to the political line of Silvio Berlusconi; from June 2007, every Friday, the periodical "Il Giornale delle Libertà" (literally "The journal of freedom"), an official organ of the Popolo delle Libertà Party, is sold with the newspaper.

In 2001 *Il Giornale* organises a media campaign dealing with the so-called Telekom Serbia case. In a 32-pages dossier, they accuse the left-wing prime minister, Romano Prodi, of having taken bribes from the Serbian President Milosevic, in order to buy a relevant quota of the Serbian national telephonic company, Telekom Serbia. The dossier was based on the statements of a witness, Igor Marini, who will be later condemned to a ten-years imprisonment for defamation and calumny.

As Giuseppe D'Avanzo recently noticed, the Telekom Serbia case is the first exemplum of how "La macchina del fango" works. Thirty two covers are consecutively dedicated to the story, with headlines like: "Telekom, 200 mld (paid) to Prodi, 150 to Fassino and 100 to Dini", or "Telekom, Dini (former Foreign Affair minister) knew he was helping Milosevic" and "Telekom, here's the proof which nails Fassino" (who was the Minister of Justice in 2001).

At the end of the story, the key witness Igor Marini was judged as not credible. The key evidence of his allegations, two orders of payment of bribes, was proved to be false, also thanks to the investigation of the left-wing newspaper *La Repubblica*.

The parliamentary committee, charged of the investigation, resigned without even presenting its final report. On November 10th, 2011, a court in Rome condemned Igor Marini to ten years of prison, for criminal association, false documents and slanders. After a three-years campaign, *Il Giornale* never mentioned about the epilogue of the story neither apologised with its readers.

"La macchina del fango" had just started to work. On August 29th, 2009, *Il Giornale* lashes out against Dino Boffo, director of L'Avvenire, a catholic newspaper who had criticised Berlusconi's immoral lifestyle. Boffo is described as a homosexual followed by the Police and as a child molester. The anonymous letter, which accused Dino Boffo, was proved to be false; meanwhile, he had resigned from its chair. Vittorio Feltri, *Il Giornale*'s director, had to serve a six-month suspension from the Order of Journalists as a penalty for Boffo's defamation.

Libero

"Younger brother" of *Il Giornale* in these "mud-racking" campaigns, *Libero* is a right-wing newspaper founded in 2000 by Vittorio Feltri.

It's driven, from August 2009, by Maurizio Belpietro (former director of *Il Giornale*).

In 2006 *Libero* published a false" dossier made by the SISMI (the Italian secret services) and signed by the vice-director Renato Farina. According to this editorial, Romano Prodi, (former left-wing Prime Minister) authorised, as President of the European Commission, '"extralegal rendition" the CIA in Europe, as in the case of Abu Omar.

Because of this false dossier, Renato Farina was sentenced to six months' imprisonment for aiding and abetting, and expelled from the Order of Journalists.

HOW THE MEDIA FRAMES POLITICAL ISSUES: "THE STRANGE CASE" OF FINI AND THE APARTMENT IN MONTECARLO.

As regards to the Italian mud-slinging machine, Alexandre Stille notices: "During the past years *Il* Giornale has raised unfounded scandals with the means to hit politic rivals. The cases of Giancarlo Caselli, or of Antonio Di Pietro, accused from 1994 to 1996 of corruption are patently clear. The newspaper had to pay € 700 million to Mr Di Pietro for their allegations" *(La Repubblica, 17 agosto 2010).*

According to the author, winner of three journalistic Awards and professor of Journalism at Columbia University in New York "*Il Giornale* has often acted as a political weapon and is used by the Premier against his rivals", in a permanent campaign that led the policy to conform to the strict logic of the market the entertainment media, in pursuit of new forms of competition, with an inescapable personalisation of leadership.

In this competition, media plays a crucial role: as Katz wrote in 1957: "When the party is the primary channel for public participation, demand aggregation and articulation, and communication from leaders to followers, party Governments will be stronger. Where other structures, e.g. mass media and interest groups, share in performing these functions, control over party politics will be weaker "(1957, p. 59).

Manuel Balàn explored the role of competition in the scandals' triggering-system. According to him, intra- government competition is the key-variable. Using his words, "where intra-government competition is strong, coalition partners are likely to seek to hurt allies by the selective leaking of information about wrong-doing as part of a strategy of leap-forging; or else, since such leaking hurts the coalition as a whole, they are likely to attempt to damage the government's reputation as part of a strategy to jump ship and join the opposition" (2011, p.9).

2010 seems to represent a turning point in the Italian political recent history. For the first time, Berlusconi's majority appears in danger because of Fini's intolerance to the PM's moral and ethical behaviour.

The relationship between the two leaders of Il Popolo della Libertà formally ends in July 2010, when the President Silvio Berlusconi de facto expels the co-founder Gianfranco Fini with a strong letter of attack.

In this document the PM Berlusconi invites Mr Fini to resign from his institutional office (the Presidency of the Deputies Chamber) because of his political positions, which are (in Berlusconi's opinion) in a deep contrast with the founding values of Il Popolo della Libertà party.

The day after the letter, Gianfranco Fini announces the birth of a new parliamentary group, composed by 34 members and called Futuro e libertà.

The third highest office of the Country digs up the hatchet of war, but without totally withdrawing his support to the Government: the new formation will support the government or not, depending on the different proposals.

The bone of contention is about the justice. A hard debate concerns a bill which dispensed the Premier from appearing to Court in a trial for corruption.

Gianfranco Fini has already criticised the government actions on the justice theme, claiming himself as sceptical about the possibility of voting such a reform of justice whose aim was to restrict freedom of press and telephone interceptions for crime investigations.

At this point of the story, the mud-slinging machine has already been turned on, as we're going to see.

In our attempt to understand the rise of this mud-slinging machine we have to refer to the concept of scandal. According to Thompson, "scandals" refers primarily to actions, events or circumstances, which have the following characteristics (2000, p.20):
- They involve the transgression of certain values, norms, or moral codes;
- They involve an element of secrecy or concealment;
- Other individuals disapprove the actions or events and may be offended by this transgression;
- The disclosure and condemnation of the actions or events may damage the reputation of the individuals responsible for them.

For many reasons – e.g. the availability of, and the incentives to acquire, compromising information, to the role of parties and their representatives in scrutiny functions and the imperatives of political competition – the likelihood is that party actors figure more prominently than other types among the instigators of scandals – that 'scandals are probably more likely to occur in politics…than in other sectors of life' (Garrard, 2005, p. 24).

Can the Fini's case be traced following this interpretative scheme? Let's try to reconstruct the story, as well as *Il Giornale* does.

To do it, we need to introduce another useful concept, that one of "mediated scandals".

As Thompson writes, "mediated scandals are a distinctive type of event which is constituted in part by mediated form of communication". These scandals "typically unfold over a period of time which is punctuated by the rithms of media organisations (...) and other institutions, such as a judicial and political institutions, which play a key role in the disclosure of information relevant to the scandal"(2000, p.72).

Following Thompson's scheme, we can reconstruct the sequential structure of Fini's scandal.

THE PRE-SCANDAL PHASE

As Thompson notices, this phase may involve the publication of information that subsequently turns out to be relevant to a scandal. It's often characterised by gossip, rumour and hearsay among political élites, journalists and others.

On September 14th, 2009, Vittorio Feltri, on a signed front-page editorial, launches the attack to the president of the Chamber of Deputies, by threatening the publishing of a red-light dossier involving members of Fini's former party, Alleanza Nazionale.

"It's better" Feltri says " let sleeping dogs lie".

An editorial that sounds like a clear warning to Gianfranco Fini. From now on, *Il Giornale* engages itself in a massive smear campaign aimed at undermining the political persona of Mr Fini and his growing popularity among the Italian electorate.

In April 2010, in conjunction with some disagreements within the majority of government, Fini is accused of having helped his mother-in-law, who heads a television production company, to obtain a one million euros contract with RAI, the public service television. The same day, Fini is defined by the same newspaper as "the virus that is wrecking the PDL".

Fini's family is introduced in the public debate. We'll see how it will be the "selling point" of the whole smear campaign.

On May 12th, 2010, Marcello Veneziani officially announces Gianfranco Fini's political suicide, due to his opposition to the Prime Minister.

Another nine political opponents share his same fate: "They die - Veneziani writes - like the ten little niggers narrated by Agatha Christie".

We can notice how *Il Giornale* has been creating the moral and political climate that allows the scandal to find space in the public media coverage of our country.

Il Giornale (and the media institution in general) contributes, to use Mc Nair's words, to policy discussion and resolution, "not only in so far as it sets public agendas or provide platforms for politicians to make its views known to the public, but also in judging and critiquing the variety of political viewpoints in circulation" (2010, p. 67).

In other words, the pre-scandal phase can be considered as functional to the imposition of the narrative framework that characterises the whole affair.

This dominant framework, as Mc Nair explains, once established, provides the structure within subsequent events are allocated news value, reported and made sense of (2010, p.68).

In this way, the permanent campaign that Sidney Blumenthal had already interpreted in a temporary key is extended in space. The assessment of the politician (in this case Fini) includes his private life, his acquaintances, his family stability.

So the climate of opinion set off by this mud-slinging campaign acts as a cognitive frame in order to facilitate the activation of the process of opinion-building in Berlusconi's permanent campaign to control the Party.

THE SCANDAL PROPER: BETWEEN A MEDIATED AND A TALK SCANDAL

The concept of mediated scandal concerns the strategical disclosure of already existing transgressions of norms and legal codes. Thompson and Tumber distinguish three types of political scandals: sexual scandals, financial scandals and power scandals (Thompson, 2000, Tumber, 2004).

In 2006 Mats Ekström and Bengt Johansson enrich the classification with a new typology: the talk scandal.

The main characteristics of these talk scandals are:

1. Utterances are manipulated to fit into headlines and dramatized news stories;
2. The risks for legal consequences are virtually non-existent.

As Ekström and Johansson underline, "the occurrence of talk scandals shows, perhaps more clearly than in any other case, that a politician's reputation and career can be seriously threatened without any existence whatsoever of the risk of legal consequences".

The process of the public disclosure of the event, in Fini's case, starts on July, the 28th, 2010.

A signed editorial on the front page of the newspaper talks about "Fini, his partner and the strange house in Montecarlo".

The article talks about an apartment in Monaco, bequeathed in 2001 by the noblewoman Anna Maria Colleoni to Alleanza Nazionale, former Fini's party.

In 2008 the party sold the flat to a mysterious offshore company, based in a tax heaven.

The charge involves Gianfranco Fini's brother in law. According to *Il Giornale*, Giancarlo Tulliani, brother of Elisabetta, the Speaker of the House's partner, would have bought the property allegedly sold at below-market value.

According to the newspaper, in fact, the offshore company registered in the Caribbean island of St Lucia, is ascribable to Tulliani Giancarlo, who now lives in the flat with a regular lease.

The whole story is not entirely told in the first editorial. The newspaper, in fact, gradually reconstructs the events, using some very effective tools.

This strategy reflects the need to keep the scandal alive. As we're going to see, this scandal takes on a dramatic character, with new occurrences every day (Lull and Hinerman, 1997).

This happens partially through revelations in the form of new facts, but an important driving force (in many cases, the most important) is all the comments that are made public daily (Ekström and Johansson, 2006).

Once the scandal begins to break, its character is shaped by the newspaper with revelations, allegations and denunciations. "The media operates as a framing device, focusing attention on an individual or an alleged activity and refusing to let go" (Thompson, p. 54).

The case of the apartment is taken up for investigation on July, 30th, when the opposite party lead by Francesco Storace laid its formal complaint.

In the attempt to build and strengthen the interpretative frame of the story, *Il Giornale* recourses to some editorial devices:

1. The **Interviews** to stakeholders, often related to the same left-wig area that launched Fini's political career. Most of them don't forgive Fini for his moderate opening after disowning his former fascist ideals.

Those figures, interviewed about the story, contribute to draw Fini's overall picture of immorality.

The classical studies on political interviews have underlined the importance of the so-called adversarial interview, whose requirement of impartiality responds to the principles of a journalism as a fourth-estate. Conversely, the role of interviews in this agenda-building strategy is merely instrumental to the dominant framework, already established by the newspaper.

As Entman noticed, one of the different news frame used by journalists in their activity is directed to the building of a moral frame (Entman, 1989).

In this case, we'll see, we assist to the gradual activation of a negative inference towards a political faction through some strategic devices.

First of all, the priming effect, which, as Sorice explains, is linked to the journalistic choice to underline or marginalise a number of subjects, thus exercising a deep influence on the personal judgment 's building process (2011, p.58).

The first person to be interviewed is Assunta Almirante, widow of Giorgio, historical leader of Msi, the post-fascist political party which Fini belonged to.

On August 4th, the old lady accuses Gianfranco Fini of high treason: he betrayed the original ideals and destroyed the Party once lead by her husband.

The other interviews' aim is to underline the general ambiguity of Fini's personal and moral behaviour. This wickedness, as we'll see later, is extended to his family, which is the root cause of the problem. As well as in Berlusconi's life, Il Giornale suggests, up to November 23rd headline: "Two women caused the political crisis". A full-page illustration shows Veronica Lario, Berlusconi's ex-wife, and Elisabetta Tulliani, Fini's partner.

In the other interviews the newspaper follows the mud-slinging strategy by investigating in Elisabetta Tulliani's past: her love stories, her family are gradually and totally laid out with embarrassing allusions about her moral "integrity".

2) The **Allusions**.

As Thompson explains, what is important in a political scandal is not so much that the actions disclosed are illegal, but rather than the norms transgressed have some degree of moral bindingness in the contest in which they are embedded. (2000, p. 120).

In general, a transgression of rules (e.g in the exercise of political power) is much more newsworthy rather than an inconvenient private conduct because of its illegal consequences.

Such a scandal is easier to be kept alive day by day. In connection with political scandals, the media is filled with comments from all possible directions – bosses, colleagues, those who stand in opposition to the person in question, family, etc.

Fini's case seems to be partially different. His alleged transgression of norms concerns the moral code, not the legal one. The apartment had been left to a political party: according to Italian constitution, parties' internal balances have no public relevance. What is necessary, for *Il Giornale*, is to extend the news frame of immorality to other, hypothetical infringements, thus assuring public expression of disapproval and guaranteeing another, crucial, mental association: all politicians have immoral behaviours. Fini can't break up with Berlusconi on the justice subject: they both broke rules, they are cast in the same mould.

This approach calls in question the soundbites effect of this strategic use of media: as Michele Sorice underlines, this campaigning method concerns "the mechanism of fragmentation and oversimplification of media political discourse whose necessary consequence is the production of political debate's oversimplification which lead to populist trivialisation"(2011, p. 56).

On August 5th *Il Giornale* begins its range of allusions: the offshore company that has bought the apartment is connected to a big gambling multinational owned by the son of a boss. So, Fini's brother in law deals with Mafia.

On August 7th, we assist to a twofold attack: on the one hand, the newspaper resumes the story of the contract signed by Fini's mother in law with Rai for a tv show. On the other hand, *Il Giornale* announces that " The prosecutors suspect other slush fund's existence".

And so on: next day here's another apartment, in Rome, left to the Party and sold to Fini's friends, on August 20th they start focusing on Elisabetta Tulliani, Fini's partner and mother his two children.

Mme Tulliani's past is inspected in detail. Like her past relationship with Luciano Gaucci, an entrepreneur condemned for bankruptcy and fugitive in Dominican Republic. On August 23rd, Luciano Gaucci accuses Elisabetta Tulliani of having stolen some properties that he had made out on behalf of her in order to prevent the seizure after the bankruptcy.

The story takes on a dramatic tone, with new occurrences every day. On September 12th an entire dossier about the Tulliani's is published. The driving force of this continue flow of information rarely involves facts; most of times, the articles are filled with rumours, comments and hearsay.

3) The **Appeal to the Public.**

As Ekström and Johansson (2006) note, this kind of scandals contain quoted voices from above to the public, and from adversary politicians ready to underline how much the behaviour of the person in question is morally reprehensible.

One of the most common questions discussed in these cases is whether or not the politician should be allowed to retain his position.

In the case of Fini, both *Il Giornale* and *Libero* organise a real mobilisation campaign in order to ask Fini's resignation.

Il Giornale decides for a signatures' gathering.

The petition officially begins on Aug. 9. *Il Giornale* publishes a front-page appeal and keeps readers constantly informed about the number of signatures received. On September 29th, the newspaper announces the achievement of 175,000 signatures.

Here's the petition's text: "Following the embarrassing story of the house in Montecarlo, bequeathed to An and finished in the hand of Fini's girlfriend's brother, we ask that the Speaker of the House immediately resign from office". Signatures can be sent via email, sms, fax or regular mail.

When the newspaper succeeds in gathering the famous people's signatures (usually directors, singers, actors), it spends entire headlines to inform its readers of the public endorsement.

A similar initiative is led by *Libero*, who decides to publish letters from its readers. In these letters, readers express their indignation and underline the hypocrisy of Fini. Everyone asks for his resignation, and accuses him of wanting to destroy the Right.

It is important to note that audience interaction is a key element of populist media: they encourage audience to show their anger and resentment, to target their elected representatives . The media and the audience they entertain are linked; they are part of the same community, sharing the same values, concerned about the same threats (ibidem) (Stayer, 2007, p. 125).

4) The attack to the **opposite newspapers**, accused of hiding the truth.

We already mentioned Italian media system partisanship, a historic framework that has been further strengthened by an entirely Italian abnormality, which concerns the ownership structure of media.

Il Giornale is in the hands of Paolo Berlusconi, brother of the Prime Minister. By the way, the newspaper has never hidden its nature of "party organ".

On the other side, the publishing group L'Espresso, which *La Repubblica* belongs to, is driven by Carlo De Benedetti, Silvio Berlusconi's historic enemy.

Decades of partisanship have given way to a declared battle. Not surprisingly, the investigation of the newspaper *La Repubblica* will be essential to reveal the structure and the lies underpinning the machine of mud. On August 6th, the first the first target to be struck is Il Corriere della Sera, the most diffused Italian newspaper: "it prevents his journalists from writing the truth", *Il Giornale* accuses. Next day here we have Repubblica, "head of justicialist and moralist Italian press", which refrains from those besiegers investigations that had showed towards Berlusconi's private life.

Other titles will end up in the crosshairs of *Il Giornale:* among them, the catholic weekly Famiglia Cristiana, L'Unità, and a tv-show, Report.

5) The **alleged statements of witnesses, often subsequently disproved by the witnesses or judicial investigation.**

In this crusade *Il Giornale* succeeds in finding several witnesses ready to confirm its version: The house in rue de la Princesse belongs to Giancarlo Tulliani and Fini knows it.

Furthermore: Fini often uses that flat, and has contributed to its furnishing.

On August, 13th, here's the first one: he's the salesman of a furniture shop in Rome, where Gianfranco Fini purchased a kitchen, which, according to *Il Giornale,* would have been shipped in the apartment in Monaco.

The "kitchen soap-opera" has just started: day after day, *Il Giornale* publishes other witnesses, who declare: "Fini was an habitué there" "I met him twice, we talked about politics", "I noticed he was there because of the police escort on the stairs" and allegations like those.

Finally, a photo of the alleged kitchen in the flat in Montecarlo is published on September, 28th. It's curious to notice that the picture has been taken by Ilaria Scavo, a journalist who works for one of the three television channels belonging to Silvio Berlusconi.

The strategic attempt is clear: in order to strengthen the moral judgment against Gianfranco Fini they need to transform moral claims into empirical claims, so that the evaluative standards used to empirically appraise the transgression seem as unambiguous as the evidence used to document existence (Ekström and Johannson).

The various allegations collected by the newspaper show how a talk scandal works. As we said before, the manipulation of utterances is one of the key features in creating and maintaining this mediated scandals.

We can find in this search for evidences an attempt to objectify a story that, otherwise, looks nothing but an attempt to slander. An increased anchoring with reality is necessary to legitimize the public condemnation and the interpretive frame of the story. Fini has lied, we have the evidences, he is no different from other politicians. Not surprisingly, "Fini as Scajola" is the headline chosen for August 9th.

These allegations are often interpretations of happenings, or hypothesis: how Patterson noticed,

"Today, facts and interpretation are freely intermixed. Interpretation provides the theme, and the facts illustrate it. The theme is primary; the facts are secondary. As a result, events are compressed and joined together within a common theme. (Gunther, Mugan, Democracies and the Media: a comparative perspective, p. 249).

The publication of incriminating documents, procured by middlemen of uncertain origin, responds to the same necessity.

The actual authenticity of such evidences, as we'll see further on, will shortly be challenged. At the same time, however, the publication of these "self-styled" documents will be the linchpin of his accusers' theory and the cornerstone that will trigger the defensive strategy of Fini.

FINI'S RESPONSE: BETWEEN IMAGE RESTORATION AND PARTY'S IDENTITY CONSTRUCTION

As Brian Mc Nair underlines, PR is "a necessary dimension of the modern political process" (McNair, 1996, p. 53).

In mediated scandal's case a PR structured response has a great importance, both in crisis management process and in public image repairing effort. The personal image of the individual can be moulded and shaped to suit organisational goals: when Montecarlo's house's scandal broke out, Gianfranco Fini's image was undergoing a process of political "institutionalisation". In his attempt to conquer the right-wing moderate votes, he had chosen a low profile strategy, against Berlusconi's excesses. Using Stein Rokkan words, he was trying to politicise the cleavage created by Berlusconi's lack of credibility and diffused in a large sector of Italian electorate.

When *Il Giornale* makes the scandal broke up, Fini has to choose a strategy for repairing his damaged image, without disowning the political turning point he had chosen to mark.

On July 30th Francesco Storace, leader of La Destra and former exponent of Alleanza Nazionale, lodges a complaint; as prescribed by the law, the prosecutors of Rome open a dossier on the affair: no-one is charged of the alleged offences.

A day later, Fini decides to sue the newspaper.

On August 8th, in a long official note, the Speaker of the House decides to intervene in order to provide his own version of the story: "When AN was in possession of the flat in Monte Carlo- Fini says- it was evaluated about four hundred million lire by the company which administered the building. The flat, how those who visited it testified, was crumbly and totally uninhabitable unless substantial restructuring costs".

Fini underlines that, unlike *Il Giornale*'s allegations, his party didn't had other formal proposals for purchasing it. Until 2008, when, as Fini admits, "Giancarlo Tulliani told me about a company interested in buying the flat".

Fini continues: "As the AN officers certified that the bid was higher than the estimated value (three hundred thousand euros against four hundred and fifty million lire) "I authorised the sale",

This procedure, Fini underlines, is the same followed in other similar cases: "Other properties inherited by Colleoni had been sold, such as a land in Monterotondo, and two others flats".

The sale of the apartment took place, according Fini's note, on "October 15th, 2008 before the notary Auréglia Caruso".

Some time later, Fini concludes, " I learned from Elisabetta his brother Giancarlo had rented the flat. My surprise and my disappointment can be easily realised".

It's important to notice how Fini's first official response comes 10 days after the scandal's explosion. This response has some fundamental features:

1. It's a written note, without any possibility of contradictory;
2. Its declared aim is to respond to another newspaper's questions, Il Corriere della Sera (the most diffused italian newspaper), which had asked him to explain the flat's case.

The choice to wait before answering has a symbolic value: as Mc Nair explains, "modern politicians are judged not only for what they say and do, but how they say and do it" (2010, p.133). This prudential approach is in line with the evolution toward moderate positions that Fini has made in his political career, from post-fascist ideals till his new political party, Futuro e Libertà per l'Italia, whose goal is to create "a European right and law-abiding" formation.

In this sense, this choice answers to a clear image management strategy: as Lees-Marshment (2004, 396) remarks, political image "is about creating a credible product that will satisfy the user in order to achieve organisational goal".

On August 13th *Il Giornale* decides to start the "kitchen soap-opera", with the testimony of an employee who claims that the furniture he sold went to decorate the house in Montecarlo.

The same day Gianfranco Fini announces a lawsuit against Vittorio Feltri, author of the editorial. At this point of the story Fini's spokesman, Fabrizio Alfano, officially comes in the debate: "What published today by *Il Giornale* is the latest demonstration of a defamatory delirium that shows how Feltri abdicated to all minimum duties of the journalist - the spin doctor says, - In order to denigrate Mr Fini, Feltri offers fictional reconstructions based on improbable stories of people who hide themselves behind anonymity: in this way the slander becomes news, and an irrelevant detail reality. The court will assess the libel, and the Council of Journalists will appraise the violation of ethical rules. "

Fini's spokesman's strategy is to deny and counteract blaming *Il Giornale*'s defamatory purpose and its attempt to use a mediated form of communication to pursue a political objective. His response comes on August 13th: at this point of the story all Italian newspaper had already taken up the story with collateral investigations. The mediated scandal had already led to both effects identified by Thompson (2000, p.84):

-first of all, a degree of homogeneity among newsworthy topics;

-then, a degree of media amplification, that had given the story greater prominence and visibility.

Along with the spokesman's note, the furniture shop hastens to officially deny his former employee's story: "Maria Teresa Castellucci's company, exercising in Rome Via Aurelia Km 13.400, with reference to the news appeared in some newspapers, claims that they never made transport or assembly of furniture from Rome to Monte Carlo, in behalf of Elisabetta Tulliani or Mr Fini".

The same pattern is repeated a few days later, on August 18th, when a new witness, an Italian businessman, comes on stage claiming he met Mr Fini outside the house in Monte Carlo, with Elisabetta Tulliani and his escort.

Again, Fini's press office responds with an official release:

"Well, a simple finding near the Italian and Monegasque authorities, which both record the movements of the escorts, would easily demonstrate that Fini's trip has never happened but in Mr. Mereto's mind. Since verifying the falsity of these statements is so easy, we all have to wonder why, those journalists who have the duty to verify the truth of news before publishing it, systematically neglects to do so".

The accusation is clear and direct: There's almost no doubt, according to Mr. Fini, that "there is, upstream, a willingness to diffuse into the news chain allegations, suspicions and accusations - even when they are spoiled by a manifest "groundlessness".

The note ends with the announcement that the Speaker of the House "will not send further denials", since he intends to provide "an accurate and detailed reconstruction of the events in court, where Feltri will be forced to give all the explanations on the case".

We can notice how, as Mc Nair argues, spin and anti-spin evolve in a dialectical relationship of action and reaction fuelled by two competing sets of communicative actors, each fighting for space in a crowded public sphere (2000).

Anyway, on the same day, Mr. Mereto disproves Feltri and accuses the newspaper of manipulating what he said:

"What reported by the journalist and in particular my alleged statements do not correspond to what I said in the presence of witnesses. I instructed my lawyers to undertake every action to safeguard my image".

Gianfranco Fini fulfills his purpose of silence until September. On September 5th, in fact, there is an important event for him. In Mirabello there is Futuro e Libertà's first convention, which marks the final break between him and Berlusconi, thus celebrating the birth of this new political subject.

Gianfranco Fini pronounces a long speech, which sounds like the founding act of his new political party.

In the speech he uses Monte Carlo story to distance himself from Berlusconi on the theme of justice. Unlike the Prime Minister, (who seeks to get immunity with laws ad personam) "We look forward to knowing the outcome of investigations. The courts will determine who is responsible for so much vulgar lies".

It's important to underline two aspects related to this speech:
- the mediated scandal against Mr. Fini breaks up in a strategical, crucial phase, when he's trying to leave Berlusconi and to form a new political team. The campaign driven by *Il Giornale* and Libero (defined "infamous" by Fini) probably accelerated the timescale and forced the Speaker of the House to match his own defence with the final attack to the Prime Minister.
- the second aspect has a more general value. As all politicians are subject to mediation, comment and interpretation by the meta-discourse of political journalism, this whole case shows how crucial is the economical factor in the production and transmission of political messages.

The disproportion between the two forces in the field is clear, but Fini is not ready to give up: "The summer campaign of some newspapers of the centre-right - he says- was the attempt to create a real Islamic stoning to death against my family," But, he argues, "we will not be intimidated by such paranoid and pathetic campaign".

The smear campaign goes on: now Gianfranco Fini is no longer an internal dissident, but a declared enemy that must be destroyed.

Two days later, on September 7th, The Speaker of the House decides to accept the first interview since the whole story started.

We have to underline that the only reactions that Fini has had during the first month charges do not involve contradictory. One hypothesis, probably the most obvious one, is that Fini has been caught unprepared by the scandal; otherwise, if we assume the existence of medium-term PR strategy, we can identify the transition from a reduce offensiveness strategy, till a veritable corrective action, two of the most known typology of common image restoration strategies (William L. Benoit, *Public Relations Review*, 1997 v23 n2).

According to Brian McNair (2003), the use of live media by skilled politicians can be an effective communicative device precisely because of its liveness and built-in uncertainty.

In this long interview granted to TgLa7, the Speaker of the House didn't dribble the questions, reaffirming he never stepped foot in that house and claiming he has nothing to do with his "brother-in-law" successive entry in the apartment, as a tenant . Anyway, he continues, "the judiciary will shed light on everything, proving the correctness of my behaviour and the unfairness of my slanderers".

This is probably the hardest proof, because of its impact on the audience of voters. Using Mc Nair's words, "the positive impact of a clear answer to a difficult question is heightened by the audience's awareness that this is, in fact, a live performance which, if probably rehearsed, cannot be edited or disguised to make it seem something which it is not. And this in the context of a public service tradition of adversarial political journalism which inclines presenters and chairmen/ women to adopt the role of devil's advocate" (2003).

In this case, the public office of the adversarial journalist is performed by Enrico Mentana, whose personal history is linked to Berlusconi's activities as a tycoon and who drives a newscast in a private Tv channel.

On September 22nd, the newspaper publishes its front page conclusive evidence:

It is a letter written by Santa Lucia's Minister of Justice and addressed to the Head of the Government of the same Caribbean island (well-known fiscal paradise), revealing that Giancarlo Tulliani "is the beneficial owner of the flat in Monte Carlo" where he lives.

The letter has been provided by Valter Lavitola, a wheeler-dealer in a close relationship with Berlusconi, who will be later arrested for extortion and lying in the induction sexy-gate that struck Berlusconi.

Three days later, on September 25th, Gianfranco Fini decides to remove all doubts and criticisms which are still being made against him. The video lasts about 14 minutes and can be divided into different sections, according to the topics covered:

1. In the first section, we have the veritable showdown with Berlusconi. Fini accuses Prime Minister to have expelled him from their party with ridiculous allegations :

since then, Fini said, "an obsessive political campaign is trying to make me resign as chairman of the House". At this point, Fini tries to mark the line of demarcation between his newborn party, FLI, and the PDL: "Obviously - he says, someone does not want to have " a right-wing party talking about the culture of legality, about men equality before the law, about guaranties that cannot means impunity, about a justice reform conceived for citizens and not for solving personal problems. "

2. The second part deals with the notion of legality, which, as we saw above, is the narrative framework chosen by Giornale and *Libero* for framing the story. Fini emphasises how he is one of the few Italian politicians in office that has never been investigated in a twenty-seven years career. The Speaker of the House underlines how, soon after receiving several warnings from the newspapers belonging to Berlusconi family, the scandal of the house broke up. And asks: was it a warning or a threat?

In any case, Fini states, "I know I owe Italian people, and not always only those who voted for me, clarity and transparency on this subject".

3. The third part is about Monte Carlo's flat. Fini confirms the story he has already told emphasising the regularity of the sale. Then he states: "As I have pointed out, only after the sale I found out that Mr. Giancarlo Tulliani was living in that house".

Finally, Fini admits: "With the wisdom of hindsight, I have to reproach myself for my naivety. But, let me be clear: no kind of crime was committed, no damage was caused to anyone. And, even more clear, in this affair the administration of public money is not involved. There are no contracts or bribes, there is no corruption or extortion".

And then the judgement: "Who is the real owner of the house in Montecarlo? Is he Giancarlo Tulliani, as many people think? I do not know".

But, Fini continues, " If it would appear with certainty that Tulliani is the owner and that my good faith has been betrayed, I would not hesitate to leave the Chairmanship ". Not for personal responsibility - that I would have - but since my public ethics would impose it to me".

4. At the end of the video Gianfranco Fini goes further: he is no longer part of Pdl. He can openly accuse Berlusconi's newspapers of leading an actual mud-slinging machine, whose consequences have repercussions the state of health and the functioning of our democracy.

"Freedom of information- he argues- is the cornerstone of a democratic and open society". But for this, newspapers and televisions can not become party tools, used not to give news and comment, but to strike at any price a political opponent". "This way, the future of freedom is undermined".

The speech ends with an appeal to all politicians: "Let's stop", because "Italians expect the legislature to continue in order to face their problems and to make their lives improved".

This speech can be considered the most complete and relevant Fini's public response about the scandal in the first three months of the case, when *Il Giornale* dedicates to the story about 90% of its front-pages.

Our description ends here. On the one hand we have seen how the mud-slinging machine worked during the first two months of its campaign against Fini, as a mean to delegitimize and smear the Speaker of the House's public image.

We saw how the mud-slinging machine has a strong structure, and how its power deeply affects the dynamics of political perception. Thus, in our country, public opinion's perception towards a candidate and her/his history is flawed by manipulating power of this kind of media that, *de facto*, turn out to be instruments of control over the entire country's political life.

Even the concept of public space, where the media exercise filtering, controlling and legitimating functions, is being challenged by mechanisms of intimidation and defamation such as the mud-slinging machine.

On the other hand we tried to reconstruct the defensive mechanism adopted by Gianfranco Fini's team, in its effort to clean up his public image and to demonstrate the inconsistency of all those allegations.

The period chosen for the analysis corresponds to the hottest phase of the story, which includes the pre-scandal and the scandal itself.

As Thompson argues, such scandals are conceived to last over time. The story of the apartment in Monte Carlo is no exception: Libero and *Il Giornale* have continued keeping the story alive with continuous, sometimes inventive, updates. As long as, on March 14th, 2011, the court of Rome dismissed the charge against Gianfranco Fini, because "there is no substance to the fact".

In our attempt to reconstruct Fini's PR strategy, we underlined how there are too many political variables in play and how Fini's restorative strategy is part of a larger project that involves his new party identity-construction process.

For this reasons, as Mc Nair argues, the only truly rational approach is to regard public relations as part of the infrastructure of modern political communication, a set of techniques and tools which are of potential value to all political actors, whether left or right, dominant or subordinate, conservative or radical.

Following this approach, Fini probably seems to emerge victorious in the struggle against the mud-slinging machine.

He managed to confirm his integrity at the very time he was launching his new political brand. He has been able to link his name to the new project, and to gather a supportive electorate around him. He succeed in the difficult task of building a relationship with his "customers" based on dialogue and sharing a common path, thus asserting a new conception of the audience, considered as an active partner in meaning-making process, as "theories of dialogue" teach.

In other words, he moulded and shaped his own image to suit organisational goal and succeed, to use James Grunig paradigm, in enhancing a good relationship between the company (the Party) and the public in order to promote its trust, commitment and satisfaction.

ONLINE REFERENCES

Balan M., *Competition by Denunciation: The Political Dynamics of Corruption Scandals in Argentina and Chile**. http://lasa.international.pitt.edu/members/congress-papers/lasa2010/files/1682.pdf

Ekström M., Johansson B. (2006), *Talk scandals,* ICA'S Annual Conference, San Fransisco. http://www.oru.se/PageFiles/24075/Talk%20scandals%20ICA%20nr%2016.pdf

http://www.youtube.com/watch?v=9AjlnkqL7Vg

http://www.youtube.com/watch?v=o5V4o8T8Vbo&feature=related

REFERENCES

Boin A., Hart P., Stern E., Sundelius B., (2005) *The politics of crisis management: public leadership under pressure,* Cambridge university press.

Caniglia E., Mazzoni M. (2011), *Nuovi approcci alla comunicazione politica,* Roma, Carocci.

Cutlip S.M. (1976). Public Relations in the Government. *Public Relations Review,* 2(2), 5-28.

De Blasio E., Hibberd M. e Sorice M. (2011) *Popular politics, populism and the leaders. Access without participation? The cases of Italy and UK,* CMCS Working Papers.

Gunther R., Mughar A., (2000) *Democracy and the Media: A Comparative Perspective*, Cambridge University Press.
Hallin D., Mancini P., (2004) *Comparing Media Systems: Three Models of Media and Politics*, Cambridge University Press.
Katz R., in Castles F. , Wildenmann R. (1986), *Visions and realities of party governments*, European University Institute.
Louw W. (2010) *The media and political process*, Sage Publications Ltd.
Mazzoleni, G. (2004), *La comunicazione politica*, Il Mulino.
McNair B., Hibberd M., Schlesinger P., (2003) *Mediated access: broadcasting and democratic participation*, University of Luton Press.
Mc Nair B., (2004) *PR Must Die: spin, anti-spin and political public relations in the UK, 1997–200* http://dl.franko.lviv.ua/medialiteracy/pr_must_die.pdf
Mc Nair B. (2011), *An introduction to political communication,* London, Routledge, .
Sabato L. (1991) *Feeding frenzy:how attack journalism has transformed American politics*, Free Press.
Saviano R, (2011) *Vieni via con me*, Feltrinelli Editore.
Sorice, M., *Comunicazione politica*, in Viganò, D. E. (a cura di), *Dizionario della comunicazione*, Carocci, 2009.
Sorice M. (2011), *La comunicazione politica*, Roma, Carocci.
Stanyer J., (2007), *Modern Political Communications: Mediated Politics In Uncertain Terms*, Polity Press.
Thompson, J.B., (2000), *Political Scandal: Power and Visibility in the Media Age*, Polity Press.

NEWSPAPERS ARTICLES

Bechis F., (2010) *Casa, Fini spieghi o lasci*. Libero, July, 31.
Belpietro M., (2010) *Fini querela ma su Montecarlo non si spiega*. Libero, August 3.
Cervo M., (2010) *La rabbia senza orgoglio di Fini*. Libero, July 31.
Chiocci G.M. (2010) *Fini, la compagna, il cognato e una strana casa a Montecarlo*. Il Giornale, July 28.
Chiocci G. M., Filippi S., (2010) *La casa di Montecarlo: ecco i conti segreti (su due società estere)*. Il Giornale, July, 30.
Cramer F., (2010) *"Fini onesto? Non ci giurerei". Intervista a Donna Assunta Almirante*. Il Giornale, August, 4.
D'Avanzo G., *Quando è nata la macchina del fango, la Repubblica*, 15 ottobre 2010.

Chiocci G.M., Lagattola E., Mattioni G., Zurlo S., (2010) *Altro testimone: Fini in quella casa*. Il Giornale, August 18.

Chiocci G.M., Malpica M., (2010) *E i pm ipotizzano anche fondi neri*. Il Giornale, August 7.

Feltri V., (2010) *Le eresie di Famiglia Cristiana*. Il Giornale, August 18.

Feltri V., (2010) *Fini non ha detto la verità. Ecco la prova*. Il Giornale, September 22.

Feltri V., (2010) *Fini, un mese di silenzi e bugie*. Il Giornale, August 28.

Feltri V., (2010), *Fini come Scajola. Raccogliamo le firme per mandarlo a casa*. Il Giornale, August 9.

Feltri V., (2010), *La prova: Fini Mente*. Il Giornale, August 13.

Foa M., (2010) *Ma guarda, i signori degli scoop sono tutti progressisti*. Il Giornale, November 30.

de' Manzoni M., (2010) *La procura indaga, Fini trema*. Il Giornale, August 5.

Sallusti A., (2010) *Il ribaltone dei finiani: alleati col Pd*. Il Giornale, September 22.

Sallusti A., (2010) *In 150mila hanno firmato per mandare a casa Fini*. Il Giornale, August 29.

Sallusti A., (2010) *Perquisita la sede di An. Il vicedirettore del Corriere: "Fini chiarisca". Ma può dirlo solo su Facebook*. Il Giornale, August 6.

Sallusti A., (2010) *Tutte le carte che accusano Fini*. Il Giornale, August 7.

Sgarbi V., (2010) *La crisi politica? È figlia di due donne*. Il Giornale, November 23.

Stille A., *Si chiama giornalismo, questo?* http://stille.blogautore.repubblica.it/2010/08/13/si-chiama-giornalismo-questo/, *La Repubblica*, 13 agosto 2010.

Stille A., *La stampa: un nervo scoperto*. http://stille.blogautore.repubblica.it/2010/08/17/la-stampa-un-nervo-scoperto/ *La Repubblica*, 17 agosto 2010.

Veneziani M., (2010), *Vi racconto la vera sindrome di Gianfranco*. Il Giornale, August 13.

Campbell, Blair and Iraq: how the spin doctor spun the spin

Elsa Pili

WHO IS ALASTAIR CAMPBELL

In our day, Alastair Campbell is a celebrity in Britain. He is not a noted singer, or the purchase of the season for Chelsea. He is not even an actor, at least not in the traditional sense, nor a politician - strictly speaking. He is a basic reference point for anyone wishing to begin a career in political communication and he has become a case study for all those who study this particular branch of communication.

Alastair Campbell has become known to the general public with the rise of the man who has long been regarded as his alter ego: Tony Blair. Two faces of same coin, one front and one behind the spotlight. Or, at least, this is the portrait of the relationship between the two that the media have painted for years and that the same Campbell, through his diaries published after retiring from the scenes of Blair, has helped fuel.

Campbell arrived at the Labour Party by the newspaper "Today", where he was political editor: the same position occupied in the newspaper "Daily Mirror" from 1989 to 1993. In those years he began to take part in the internal construction of the party through his friendship with Neil Kinnock, Labour Secretary from 1983 to 1992, with whom he shared the holidays and of which he was close advisor. Kinnock is now commonly regarded as the precursor of "New Labour", the initiator of a deep process of modernization within the party: a legacy that Campbell has collected and brought to fruition during the rise of Tony Blair and their years at government.

At the time of "Today" he participated in the creation of interviews with three candidates to the secretary of the Labour Party in 1994, after the sudden death of John Smith, Margaret Beckett, John Prescott and Tony Blair. Although even then there was a link between the two, and despite the contribution of Campbell on the construction of the "modernizers" current within the Labour Party was significant and helped to bring victory to Blair, the professional relationship between them began officially with the conquest of the party secretariat, when Campbell became Blair's spokesman. After Blair's victory at the general elections of 1997, he became Prime Minister's chief press secretary and then, in 2000, he took the role of Prime Minister's Director of Communications, with special powers that until then had never been assigned to a political advisor who was not elected by the people.

What being a spin-doctor means

The term "spin doctor" seems to derive from baseball where a player can impart spin effect to the ball to direct it in a favorable direction and it is used to indicate a professional figure who interprets and presents to the media in a positive way the words and actions of major public personalities - in this case, political actors.

The term was born in the U.S. during the '80s. One of the first times that was used was during the presidential elections of 1984, in an article in The New York Times: «A dozen men in good suits and women in silk dresses will Circulate smoothly among the reporters, spouting confident opinions. They will not be just press agents trying to impart a favorable spin to a routine release. They'll be the Spin Doctors, senior advisers to the candidates».

Trying to place the profession of spin doctor in the macro area of political communication, it could be defined as a specific variation of the broader concept of *media management*, which in turn falls within the major category of *public relations*.

For Brian McNair media management «comprises activities designed to maintain a positive politician-media relationship, acknowledging the needs which each has of the other, while exploiting the institutional characteristics of both sets of actor for maximum advantage. For the politicians, this requires giving the media organization what it wants, in terms of news or entertainment, while exerting some influence over how that something is mediated and presented to the audience» (McNair, 2007; p. 121). The author describes spin doctors as «public relations professionals, whose job is to attempt to ensure that the interpretation of a speaker's words (or gaffes) is a convenient and desirable one. These 'spin doctors' seek to shape the journalistic agenda in making sense of their employers' discourse. This they may do by issuing press releases clarifying ambiguous or contradictory remarks, having quiet words with key journalist and pundits or giving news conferences» (McNair, 2007; p. 130).

In recent years the concept of "spin doctor" has, however, crossed the barriers of the professional role of mediator between the original utterance and image of the politician and their adoption by the media (and especially the transmission to the public) and it can now be defined as «the collecting point of a range of communication activities carried out by very articulate teams of specialists who are looking for a consensus even from a proper sociological analysis of emergencies and more widespread social demands» (Sorice, 2011; p. 80). This wider interpretation of the figure of the spin doctor is particularly suited to the case of Alastair Campbell. Over time, in fact, he earned an ever-increasing power that from the management of communication extended to the content level of policy choices. This is due, in large part, of his close relationship with Blair as well, of course, the extraordinary results obtained with its help, first and foremost the creation of New Labour.

New Labour: a revolution between form and content

It is not an easy task to describe in few words what it was New Labour, or at least how it presented itself to the voters. Political implementation of a much broader and comprehensive project that Anthony Giddens postulated in his theory of "Third Way", the New Labour, as many of his admirers and critics found themselves oddly enough to agree, featured more in negative than positive, more for what "it was not" that for what it actually was. Philip Gould, pollster and strategic advisor, another key figure in Blair's "Inner Circle", described New Labour as «genuinely radical in its approach to politics, and its beliefs are often rooted in paradox: it is pro-business and yet anti-poverty; it want taxes down for people who work hard, but public expenditure up for health and education; it seeks to be tough on both crime and its causes» (Gould, 1999; Preface, XI).

David Marquand, British academic and Labour MP 1966-77, described New Labour with a significantly more critical tone: «New Labour dilated endlessly on what it was not. It insisted ad nauseam that it was not 'Old Labour', but that was another term of art, baffling to the uninitiated. It denied that it was Thatcherite. It was not Eurosceptic, but it was not in favour of a federal Europe. It had no plans to re-nationalise the undertakings that the Conservatives had privatized. It was not corporatist. Nor was it socialist in any recognizable sense. Instead it was 'social-ist', a Blair coinage explicitly designed to 'liberate' the party from its history. It professed no ideology. 'What counts' its election manifesto proclaimed, 'is what works'. It did not identify itself with any class or interest group. With resounding banality, it claimed to stand 'for the many and not for the few'. Like virtually all political movements in modern democracies, it was for equality of opportunity, but it was not egalitarian in any stronger sense» (Marquand, 2008; p. 356), adding that «the label, 'New' Labour, was the symbol and guarantee of their victory over the rest of the party. It was also a symbol of Blair's victory – a blank sheet on which he could write whatever he wished» (Marquand, 2008; p. 358).

In fact, there was a limit to what Blair and New Labour could write on that blank sheet of paper, which soon manifested itself in all its dangerous evidence. This constant presence of ideal references belonging to traditions a long time antithetical, which represented the greatest challenge for the sealing of an internal coherence to the party, finds its emblematic example in the episode subject of this essay: the participation of a Labour government in a war that the commentators, the British people and especially the Labour electorate have never believed to be a defensive war.

CONTEXT: A WAR WITHOUT ITS CASUS BELLI

After the terrorist attack on the Twin Towers on September 11th 2001, the United States considered themselves under attack and officially proclaimed the "war on terrorism". The first target chosen was Afghanistan, considered refuge of the Islamic military organization Al-Qaeda, which had officially claimed responsibility for the attack on September 11th. After only a few months of fighting, with the Afghan campaign still in full swing, in January 2002 President George W. Bush, on the occasion of the State of the Union speech, extended the attention of the United States to other countries which he identified as dangerous to U.S. security and described as "axis of evil": Iran, Iraq and North Korea. A few months later, he enunciated the "Bush doctrine", in which the concept of preventive war had great significance («If we wait for threats to fully materialize, we will have waited too long — Our security will require transforming the military you will lead — a military that must be ready to strike at a moment's notice in any dark corner of the world. And our security will require all Americans to be forward-looking and resolute, to be ready for preemptive action when necessary to defend our liberty and to defend our lives») as the commitment to "export democracy" («Wherever we carry it, the American flag will stand not only for our power, but for freedom. Our nation's cause has always been larger than our nation's defence. [...] We wish for others only what we wish for ourselves – safety from violence, the rewards of liberty, and the hope for a better life»)[1]. In this way, with the battle still going on in Afghanistan, it was decided to attack Iraq to depose Saddam Hussein and prevent the use of hypothetical weapons of mass destruction in his possession: on March 20th 2003 a coalition led by the United States, in which Great Britain was the main ally, invaded the country. But while Bush was easier to present to his own nation the need to attack Iraq and get a strong (though not unanimous) support from American citizens still marked by memories of the gash that the tragedy of September 11th had irreparably etched in their minds, for Blair it was

---

1 georgewbush-whitehouse.archives.gov

much more complex, as Marquand explains: «Bush had no qualms about saying that his purpose in going to war was to topple Saddam [...] Blair could not afford to say that out loud. War for regime change would break international law and would not win UN approval. If he tried to take Britain into a war fought avowedly for regime change, he would split his party and court defeat in Parliament. From his point of view, it was politically essential to disguise what was in fact a war for regime change as a war to preempt an imminent threat. If humanly possible, he also had to win UN support for it» (Marquand, 2008; p. 391). Tony Blair had no luck with the United Nations, who denied approval for the war, but certainly could not afford to conduct a war without the consent of his party and British population; therefore he gave intelligence mandate to prepare two dossiers outlining the situation in Iraq and the degree of threat posed to Britain. As McNair explained, «the presentation of the dossiers was intended by the government to secure both public and parliamentary support behind the decision to invade. Such support was extended by MPs to Tony Blair in the House of Commons, largely on the basis of their acceptance of his argument that Iraq presented a real and immediate threat to British, Western and global interests. A majority of the British public also supported the invasion, although many did not, and protest against the war took place in London and Glasgow, as well as in many other European cities in February and March 2003. Without this parliamentary and public support, mobilized not least by impassioned speeches by Tony Blair himself, Britain's participation in the invasion would not have been possible» (McNair, 2007; p. 182).The first dossier, "Iraq's Weapons of Mass Destruction: The Assessment of the British Government", was published on September 24th 2002 and it contained that which soon became the famous assertion that Iraq «continued to produce chemical and biological agents» and that «some of these weapons are deployable within 45 minutes of an order to use them»[2]. The second one, "Iraq: Its Infrastructure of Concealment, Deception and Intimidation", was issued to journalists by Alastair Campbell on February 3rd 2003. Within the next few months an incredible storm would break out.

HOW TO LOSE A HUGE CREDIT OF TRUST IN LESS THAN 12 MONTHS (AND HOW TO REGAIN IT?)

On May 29th 2003, during a BBC Radio 4 Today program, Andrew Gilligan, a BBC reporter, claimed that an anonymous source from the intelligence had told him that the Government had "sexed-up" September dossier and «probably knew that the 45 minute figure was wrong even before it decided to put it in». The same day Gavin Hewitt on the Ten O'Clock News reported the same accusation, as Susan Watts would do on her News night program on June 2nd. On June 1st Gilligan wrote an article for The Mail on Sunday on the same subject while switching to a quite general allegation to a very specific one: he specifically named Alastair Campbell as the direct responsible for entering information about the 45 minutes against the advice of intelligence. Considering the gravity of the charges, the Foreign Affairs Select Committee was given the task of conducting an inquiry about "The Decision to Go to War in Iraq".

The first reaction from the government was entrusted to Tony Blair's official spokesman, who, noting that both the Prime Minister and John Scarlett (the head of the Joint Intelligence Committee) strongly denied the accusations of intelligence manipulation made by Gilligan, spoke of the Gilligan's report as containing «a number of inaccuracies». On the same occasion it appears the first response strategy carried out by Downing Street, which was to deny the importance of the accused statement: «The Government also published evidence showing that the claim over the "45 minutes" threat had not been a repeated justification for war. It was mentioned in the Commons only once by Mr Blair ahead of military action» (Baldwin, Kite; June 6).

Meanwhile, Blair and his staff were preparing to face, over the attack of the BBC and the accusations that he carried out his own country in a war without just cause, the "friendly fire" of a part of Labour Party and particularly of former members of his group which revolted against him: Robin Cook and Claire Short both resigned because of the decision to go to war and they were called to give evidence to the FAC. Claire Short said that «Tony Blair bypassed his Cabinet and took the country to war in Iraq based on decision taken by a small group of unelected advisers» adding that «this is quite a collapse in the normal procedures for decision-making. It was only the close entourage who were really part of this». Cook concentrated his evidence on the dossiers: «there was a striking absence of any recent and alarming firm intelligence. The great majority was derivative», declaring then that he thought «it would be fair to say there was a selection of evidence to support a conclusion» (Charter; June 18).

During the analysis of dossiers by the FAC, but above all by the media, it was discovered that the document in February – presented by Tony Blair and Colin Powell with enthusiastic tone and praised as an important intelligence research – was in fact, largely a plagiarism of a paper by a PhD student found on the internet and, of course, not mentioned in the document. It was evident the threat of a tremendous loss of credibility and trust for the Government, though, as Peter Riddell wrote in The Times, «this is damaging to Blair on the "trust" issue, but is secondary to, and a distraction from, the central question of whether the Government exaggerated intelligence» (Riddell; June 25).

On June 25th, Campbell was called to give evidence in front of the FAC. On this occasion he made crystal clear the strategy chosen to address what might be called "Iraq-gate": abandon the defence and switch to a ferocious attack. He did not attempt to defend himself against charges that he had "sexed up" the dossier, instead he raised the stakes by saying that the BBC had not only lied but that they lied voluntarily to carry on their anti-government and anti-war politics. So he alleged that BBC own apologies to him and Tony Blair. «I simply say in relation to the BBC story – it is a lie» he said, adding that in the run-up to the conflict «there was an agenda in large parts of the BBC... there was a disproportionate focus upon the dissent, the opposition to our position» (Webster, Charter; June 26). He continued saying «this is about as serious an allegation you can make, not just against me but against the Prime Minister and the intelligence agencies. They are basically saying that they took the country into conflict with all that entails with the loss of life, on the basis of a lie». He admitted he «had made drafting suggestions» on the September dossier, as did Blair, but his were only on «presentational issues», adding that «the PM's suggestions, and mine, were for the JIC chairman to accept or reject as he saw fit». He tried to return to the first dossier whenever he had the opportunity to divert attention from the so-called "dodgy dossier" of February, which was drafted by a team under his direct control. He, however, admitted the error of not recognizing the original text of the PhD student and added that he was «happy to send him an apology on behalf of the whole communication team of No 10» (Charter; June 26). Compliant and gentle, in this way Campbell has highlighted the difference in attitude with respect to the two dossiers: ready to admit his mistakes if he was wrong but aggressive and determined when he knew that he had acted properly. Apologizing for the February dossier meant, automatically, to gain credibility in describing the BBC's allegations about the dossier of September as a lie. The next day Campbell went on with his strategy of pressure: «The government bombarded the BBC throughout the day with demands for an apology and immediate answers to a host of questions surrounding its claim that Downing Street exaggerate the case against Iraq in the run-up to war [...] The Government's assault on the BBC yesterday began with 11 questions from Mr Blair's official spokesman at Downing Street's morning briefing [...], the spokesman released a letter from Mr Campbell to Richard Sambrook, the Director of News, largely repeating the morning's questions and adding another batch». Greg Dyke, the BBC Director General, vowed to stand firm against «unprecedented pressure» from Blair and Campbell and «personally authorised a fiercely-worded statement rejecting Mr Campbell's demand for answers by midnight to a range of questions on the BBC's conduct» (Pierce, Charter, Baldwin; June 27). A few days later Campbell announced he would organize a protest, to which he wished Labour MPs would have adhered, to ask every single BBC program that has brought forward the accusation that him and the Government had "sexed up" the dossiers to apologize. If that did not work, he promised he would have made a formal complaint to the Broadcasting Standards Commission. Sambrook wrote a long reply to him, based on three points: he rejected the accusation that the BBC had an anti-war attitude, since the tortures and political repression made by Saddam's regime were shown in many services, then, the BBC has shown a strong concern about September dossier only in light of the findings on the February dossier, finally, that the BBC was not the only one to take forward these allegations but many other titles did so. But Campbell did not move a step from his position: «I do not want 12 pages of weasel words, sophistry and a defence of unethical journalism. Far better would be a 12-word apology that says 'The BBC allegation were wholly false and we apologize sincerely for them'» (Webster, Charter, Baldwin, Bennett; June 28).

While in the newspapers and on television screens a tireless repartee between Campbell and the heads of the BBC kept on, the conclusions of the FAC's inquiry was coming closer and it became increasingly obvious a truth so far neglected: «If, as seems likely, Mr Campbell is cleared of inserting the claim that Iraq's WMD were 45 minutes from being deployed, that did not answer the wider question whether the Government exaggerated the case for war» (Snoddy, Sherwin, Charter; June 30). The focus was clearly shifting to another subject, of which Campbell was a shield until that moment: Tony Blair. The centre of attention was no longer the single statement about the 45 minutes or even the presence of weapons of mass destruction in Iraq. Perhaps it was no longer even the participation of Britain in a war it did not belong. To be questioned, every day more, was the whole mode of the Blair government: the undisputed reign of political advisors over civil servants, the merger between the structures of government and those of the party, the strong centralization and verticalization of the power he had imposed. Campbell's strategy was risky: his determination against the BBC and the aggressiveness of his tone did not go unnoticed, and some commentators pointed out the dangerous game that definitively put at risk the credibility of the Government: «Before he gets too carried away, Campbell should bear in mind that questions that resonate within the Westminster village do not always have the same effect on the British public. If he goes on banging away in the way that he has been doing, my guess is that – whatever the finding of the Commons Foreign Affairs Select Committee – all he will have succeeded in doing is widening the Government's credibility gap» (Howard; July 1).

On July 7th, the final report of the FAC was published, preceded, the day before, by a letter signed by 11 members of the Board of Governors of the BBC where the top of the television company sided firmly with Gilligan and reasserted their approval for the rules and procedures adopted in the transmission of news about the dossier (The Times, July 7). The report of the FAC was not, in fact, conclusive: MPs split along party lines on some key points, undermining the impact of it, and all the members complained not having had access to some key documents produced by the Joint Intelligence Committee. However, Campbell was cleared of the accusation he had exercised improper influence over the drafting of the dossier, while the February dossier was unanimously criticized as «almost wholly counterproductive» because of the presence of plagiarized material: «by producing such a document the Government undermined the credibility of the case for war» (Charter; July 8).

Downing Street did not find, therefore, great comfort in the judgment of the Committee, as the report itself implicitly stated in its conclusions: «continuing disquiet and unease about the claims made in the September dossier are unlikely to be dispelled unless more evidence of Iraq's weapons of mass destruction programmes comes to light» (Riddell; July 8). Campbell was no longer on centre stage but the strategy of attack that he had put up against the BBC had only resulted in exposing even more Tony Blair and his government. The fight with the BBC had ended up weakening both the Government and the broadcast company, causing a collapse in both institutions in terms of credibility: «As the Times/Populos poll published today indicates, voters are irritated by its [the Government's] performance at present and, in part because of the failure to uncover any biological and chemical arsenals in Iraq, inclined to think that the Prime Minister is not entirely trustworthy, while wondering whether the war to oust Saddam was worthwhile» (The Times; July 8).

On July 9th there was a turn of events: the Ministry of Defence announces that one of his employees admitted having spoken to Gilligan: «the adviser […] is not a member of the intelligence services and was not, as the BBC has claimed about its source, "one of the senior officials in charge of drawing up the dossier" […] the MoD said that the adviser had helped to draft a section of the dossier, but he had never been given access to raw intelligence nor been involved in discussions about what should be included in other sections». The MoD added that «when Mr Gilligan asked about the role of Alastair Campbell with regard to the 45-minute issue, he made no comment and explained that he was not in the process of drawing up the intelligence parts of the dossier. He says he made no other comment about Mr Campbell. When Mr Gilligan asked him why the 45-minute point was in the dossier he commented that it was 'probably for impact'» (Baldwin, Evans; July 9). The next day the name of David Kelly already appeared in the newspapers. Geoff Hoon, Defence Secretary, wrote to the BBC naming Dr Kelly and asking for confirmation, but the BBC did not answer. The FAC reopened its inquiry, proceeding in the hearing of Dr Kelly on July 15th and on July 17th of Gilligan again. The general political climate had become tense and permeated with distrust: «Ian Duncan Smith accused Mr Blair of becoming a "stranger to the truth". The Tory leader said that the Prime Minister and Alastair

Campbell, the No 10 communications director, had created "a culture of deceit and spin" in government» (Webster, Charter; July 17). It was not the first time that the Labour leader and, above all, his spin doctor were facing similar criticism. But this time the affair was more serious: it was not "directing the public opinion" on matters of domestic policy, dozens of young British soldiers were dying in Iraq and the sense of this human sacrifice, for those waiting for them at home, was fading more each day. Within a few days the seriousness of the issue would be raised again, taking dramatic implications and bringing the Blair Government in one of the most difficult post-war crisis in Britain's history. Tony Blair gave a passionate and compelling speech to U.S. Congress on July 17th and the comments of the FAC, that after hearing Gilligan for the second time judged him an "unsatisfactory witness who kept changing his story", seemed to foreshadow Campbell and the Government can breathe a first sigh of relief. Unfortunately, the tragedy was just around the corner.

On the morning of July 18th, David Kelly was found dead near his country house in Oxfordshire. «Mr Campbell immediately returned to his North London home, where he remained for the rest of the day. He had been irritated by the regular presence of photographers on his doorstep over the past month, but yesterday he was greeted home by a pack of 30. Although he prides himself on a tough, uncompromising image, friends of Downing Street's "king spin" said he was genuinely shaken by Dr. Kelly's death. [...] "If Alastair had known it was going to end like this he would have decided the BBC's story wasn't worth a candle", one said. "He feels that he has done nothing wrong and has told the truth throughout. But this shows something has gone horribly wrong with our political and media culture"» (Baldwin; July 19). As events unfolded, Gilligan constantly changing version, several people from the BBC intervening and all newspapers speaking of the circumstances of the death of Dr. Kelly, the pressures he might have suffered and his mental situation, one thing probably became increasingly clear for Campbell: Blair was now in a seriously dangerous position and there was no space for playing anymore, they had to review priorities. The first one had to be Blair himself.

Blair and Campbell were fighting on three different battlefields: the first against the intelligence, which the government accused of having produced unreliable information and which in turn accused the government of having «sexed up» intelligence information; the second fight was inside the Labour Party, where a significant group appealed to the pacifist tradition of the party and flaunted a war without justification, moreover fought alongside a neoconservative America; the third battle was also the most spectacular, against that BBC that Campbell wanted desperately prove to be in error.

On July 20th, Sambrook officially revealed that Dr. Kelly was the source of the charged report. Blair and Campbell heaved a sigh of relief and the Prime Minister intervened with a clear conciliatory intent: «Whatever the differences, no one wanted this tragedy to happen. I know that everyone, including the BBC, have been shocked by it. The independent Hutton Inquiry has been set up, it will establish the facts. In the meantime our attitude should be one of respect and restraint, no recrimination, with the Kelly family uppermost in our minds at this time» (Webster, Snoddy; July 21).

The Hutton Inquiry, set up to ascertain the circumstances of the death of Dr. Kelly, began its work in August and at the end of July Campbell officialised his intention to resign. Intention he had already communicated to the Prime Minister in April but that he had to put aside due to the outbreak of Iraq affair. The polls were not encouraging: from 17-point lead over Tories just 18 months before, the Labour Party was now just 2 points above. Disillusioned voters showed the perception of being led «by a Prime Minister who is a "spinner" extraordinaire. A stress on spin is common to all governments, and to virtually every company, but the Blair government has been so successful at massaging the message that the public is now tempted to disbelieve everything» (The Times, July 28). Blair, confirming the attitude of condescension described previously, did not hide and he admitted this loss of confidence, and promised to dialogue with British people and provide them with all necessary explanations: «There is an issue that we have to confront. People need to know that what we did in Iraq was right and justified. That's a case we have not just to assert, but prove over time, both in relation to weapons of mass destruction and in relation to the improvement of Iraq» (Bennett; July 31). All this happened despite, during hearings before the Hutton Inquiry, BBC admitted several pieces of material errors in the transmission of news that had triggered the conflict, including Today's editors said that Gilligan's story was «marred by flow reporting» and Gilligan himself, who «agreed that some of his reporting had not been perfect» (Webster; August 13). The fact that, despite the Government's position regained authority, public confidence remained very low, is evidence of how the problem had by now assumed proportions that exceeded those of the individual case file or the death of Dr. Kelly, taking his own life. As William Rees-Mogg in the Times explained clearly, under Tony Blair «the whole government information service was politicized. Alastair Campbell moved from being the chief Labour party propagandist to being the head of the government information service. He did not give up propaganda. As a consequence the government information service ceased to be trustworthy; it was no longer a Civil Service system but a party system. [...] Spin has destroyed trust. The need for the Hutton Inquiry itself arose because trust had been destroyed». The author pointed out only one solution: «to return to the old dividing line between the parties and the civil servants, between propaganda and information» (Rees-Mogg; August 18). This problem of confusion between the party and civil servants is raised in many other articles during the Hutton Inquiry, a clear sign that the finger was pointed at not only what happened, but especially at the way in which the different actors used to act.

Throughout this time the voice of Campbell disappeared almost entirely: the decision to go on holiday in the middle of the Hutton Inquiry, furthermore announcing he did not know whether he would return to his office once he would be back, seemed a pretty clear signal of a low-profile strategy. Presumably at this point it became clear to Campbell that being the centre of the investigation meant dragging with him also his boss, who ended up being the main prey. If the damage for him to be judged as a manipulator of information was not too serious (after all, it was not far from what he was blamed of for all his life) he knew that a Prime Minister could not face charges of having led his country through deception in an unjustified war in which dozens of British soldiers died. He undertook, therefore, in regaining credibility: not his own but Tony Blair's one. As Rod Liddle wrote at the end of August, «the problem for the Prime Minister is the extent to which he and his dispossessed chief of communications are seen by a dissatisfied electorate as indivisible: as being, in effect, one and the same creature» (Liddle; August 30). The risk was that that a general discontent began to emerge also towards the actions of domestic policy and Blair, deprived of his words' magicians and stripped of every dialectical artifice, found himself alone, facing the people: «The real problem with this Government was never Campbell, nor the ministers, the advisers, the spin or war in Iraq. Or, rather, it was all of them, but only in so far as they represented the will of Tony Blair. For the real problem of this Government is the Prime Minister. Never has Mr Blair had a clear agenda for office. Never has New Labour stood for more than not being old Labour. And never is that truer than today» (Miles; September 3).

Campbell strategy became clear during his testimony at the Hutton Inquiry, on July 19th, where he read excerpts from his diary and painted a perfect portrait of a wise Blair: he said that in his fight with the BBC he was «too angry» and he talked about a «mounting sense of anger and frustration that it was becoming impossible to deal with this» (Kennedy; August 20), and he said Blair ordered him to stop it: «He said this was clearly an intense row. You can keep going but after a day or two you should leave this to the committee [the FAC]». Blair, in Campbell's reconstruction, showed the same attitude of caution about the opportunity to make public or not the name of David Kelly: «If it came out at the weekend, we might be accused of a cover-up on the eve of the FAC report" he said, but added that the Prime Minister told him to "leave it" to the MoD. "I did not agree at the time"[...] By July 9th, Mr Campbell said his diaries suggested the big thing needed to prove the BBC allegations false was disclosure of Dr. Kelly's name. But he told the inquiry: "I did not do anything to bring that about because I was under strict instruction not to"» (Baldwin; August 20). His attitude during the hearing was completely different from the one that made him famous: «we were presented with a careful, methodical Campbell, who acknowledged that key elements of the David Kelly tragedy should have been handled differently by the Government. His answers were studded with "My Lords" and "Sirs", as he told the Hutton Inquiry that it would be been better for the Government to have named Dr. Kelly soon after the scientist came forward [...] His appearance was an exercise in self-restraint» (The Times; August 20). Meanwhile, the Hutton Inquiry was in possession of an explosive memo that highlighted the close relationship of dependence between Blair and Campbell: «this memo shows Mr Campbell telling the Prime Minister exactly what to say in the Commons on June 4th, his first parliamentary appearance after the row with the BBC erupted. As well as providing all the lines, Mr Campbell also issues instructions on the Prime Minister's demeanor at the dispatch box. [...] The memo provides plenty of ammunition for those who suspect that in the relationship between the Prime Minister and his communications director, it is Mr Campbell who wears the trousers» (Bennett; August 25). Paradoxically this was the great danger of the Hutton Inquiry: during its deployment many confidential documents were made public. That shifted the focus from Iraq to the relationship between Blair and Campbell and, more generally, the management of No 10, whose portrait looks «more like a court than a hierarchical organization» (Riddell; September 4). On August 28th it was Blair's turn before the Hutton Inquiry, and he showed a great sense of responsibility and caution in his decisions: «The responsibility is mine, at the end of the day. I take the decision as Prime Minister but I wanted to be able to say that we had played by the book» (Charter; August 29). Blair told, then, about his sense of unease about the battle with the BBC and Campbell's approach: «To be blunt about it, I thought we had to move on». He tried to call Gavyn Davies, the Chairman of the BBC, «to see if there was some way we could find a way through this» and suggested the BBC could stand by its right to have broadcast the story but accepting it was wrong. He had a negative response (Baldwin; August 29).

At the end of the holidays Campbell quit his job and Blair greeted him describing him as «able, fearless, loyal servant of the cause he believed in [...] He was, is and will remain a good friend» (The Times; August 30). To take the place of Campbell was called David Hill, the former Labour press chief, and it was also announced that a Permanent Secretary in the Cabinet Office would had handle the general supervision of the organization with the media. The purpose was so obvious that it could not escape the newspapers: «The Prime Minister will use the resignation of Alastair Campbell yesterday to re-launch the Government and attempt to win back public trust by promising a clean break with spin» (Bennett, Baldwin; August 30).

At the end of September, Campbell authorized the Hutton Inquiry for using of excerpts from his diaries. On one hand, during his evidence he was not afraid to show his animus against the BBC, on the other hand, in his diary a portrait emerged of a cautious and conscientious Tony Blair, who insisted on the need to properly follow the MoD procedures in the management of the identity of David Kelly: «Mr Campbell will be seen by many to have performed a last service for Mr Blair by acting as a lightning conductor for him» (Webster; September 23).

Campbell's last appearance in 2003, after a long absence from the scene and with a completely renovated image, was at the annual dinner of the Foreign Press Association, when he sided in favour of democracy and "good" politics, against cynicism of the media: «Scepticism is healthy. Cynicism is not. And the relentless, often 24-hour degrading of politics, politicians and anything they may have to say or do does nobody any good, including the media» (The Times; November 26).

CONCLUSIONS

This work does not pretend to account for the entire development of the Iraq affair, nor to explain the change of internal balances at Blair government nor in the British public opinion. The dispute about the need for Britain to go to war and the use of spinning techniques more or less manipulative of public opinion will continue well beyond the events considered in this paper and the Hutton Inquiry itself, which will be followed in 2009 by the Chilcot Inquiry, concluded only a year ago and to which Campbell himself was called to give evidence in 2010.

In my analysis I considered a finite period of time (year 2003) and, as a source, a single newspaper, The Times. Firstly because it is the second newspaper by circulation after the Daily Telegraph and then because I believed that the mix between Rupert Murdoch's ownership - who has always shown a sympathy for Tony Blair - and its conservative tradition would make it a complete source able to offer different points of view on the events examined. I must say this was exactly what happened: in all phases I found articles distinctly in support of Campbell and Blair (Tom Baldwin in particular) and others very critical.

What I tried to do with this analysis was, starting from basic information about the context and the characters involved, to take a picture of a moment of deep crisis, both of image and credibility, which involved two major players: Alastair Campbell and Tony Blair. Campbell was the first to come under investigation on charges of having "sexed up" the dossier that supported British intervention in Iraq, but because of the close relationship between the two, Blair was soon dragged to centre stage too. When Campbell realized that he had become the greatest danger for Blair he suddenly dropped his aggressive strategy to adopt more subdued tones and began to move backwards until he disappeared, not without having first pointed out in every possible occasion how Blair was absolutely contrary to his suggestions both on the row with the BBC and on the opportunity to make public the name of David Kelly. He never bothered to deny he was the bad guy in that story, while he always had as his first concern to emphasize that Blair was definitely the good one, the one who believed in what he did and did it for the good of his people.

Brian McNair wrote: «Modern wars are as much about communication as armed aggression. In a liberal democracy, where government must submit itself to periodic electoral judgement, wars, to a greater extent than any other aspect of policy, must be legitimized in the eyes of the people» (McNair, 2007; p. 182). A spin doctor works with words and concepts and can hardly place weapons of mass destruction where there are none (or, at least, where they can not be found). But he can, as in this case, manage to legitimate a Prime Minister who led his country into a war that that his country itself has never legitimized.

A strategic operation of full recovery of credibility that has allowed Tony Blair not to lose the general election of 2005 and earned him his third term as Prime Minister of Britain.

REFERENCES

Campbell Alastair. (2008) *The Blair's years*. London: Arrow Books.
Gould Philip. (1999) *The Unfinished Revolution*. London: Abacus.
Marquand David. (2009) *Britain since 1918*. London: Phoenix - Orion Books.
McNair Brian. (2007) *An introduction to political communication*. Abingdon: Routledge.

The Times, articles from January 2003 to December 2003

Bennett, R. (2003) *Blair admits loss of trust over Iraq*. The Times, July 31st; p. 2.
Bennett, R. (2003) *Campbell told Blair to calm the frenzy on Iraq*. The Times, August 25th; p. 11.
Bennett, R. and T. Baldwin. (2003) *The end of Labour's spin cycle?*. The Times, August 30th; p. 1.
Baldwin, T. (2003) *Dossier rivals retreat 'shaken and sickened'*. The Times, July 19th; p. 6.
Baldwin, T. (2003) *The secret diary of Alastair Campbell aged 46 and a bit*. The Times, August 20th; p. 11.
Baldwin, T. (2003) *Buck stops here for leader with keen eye on his image*. The Times, August 29th; p. 13.
Baldwin, T. and M. Kite. 2003. No 10 points to new BBC 'errors'. The Times, June 6; p. 16.

Baldwin, T. and M. Evans. (2003) *MoD man admits: I spoke to the BBC.* The Times, July 9th; p. 2.

Charter D. (2003) *How Blair and his aides 'left Cabinet behind' on road to war.* The Times, June 18th; p. 4.

Charter, D. (2003) *'They are saying we took the country into conflict on the basis of a lie'.* The Times, June 26th; p. 12.

Charter, D. (2003) *Campbell mistaken but not improper.* The Times, July 8th; p. 10.

Charter, D. (2003) *'I wanted to say we had played by the book'.* The Times, August 29th; p. 13.

Howard, A. (2003) *We should remember the old adage: opposition do no twin elections, government lose them.* The Times, July 1st; p. 3.

Kennedy, D. (2003) *Blair tried to cool "sexed-up" row with the BBC.* The Times, August 20th; p. 11.

Liddle, R. (2003) *Would you really believe anything that he told you?.* The Times, August 30th; p. 6.

Miles, A. (2003) *You cannot govern with a light hearth, Mr Blair.* The Times, September 3rd; p. 20.

Pierce, A., D. Charter and T. Baldwin. (2003) *BBC and Blair plunged into war 'lies' crisis.* The Times, June 27th; p. 1.

Rees-Mogg, W. (2003) *Campbell, a new model Cromwell for our age.* The Times, August 18th; p. 16.

Riddell, P. (2003) *Rising death toll poses tougher questions than MPs' inquest.* The Times, June 25th; p. 4.

Riddell, P. (2003) *Row has only fuelled doubt about the war.* The Times, July 8th; p. 11.

Riddell, P. (2003) *Yes, Prime Minister takes over the West Wing.* The Times, September 4th; p. 22.

Snoddy, R., A. Sherwin and D. Charter. (2003) B*BC seeks go-between to sue for peace with Labour.* The Times, June 30th; p. 1.

Webster, P. (2003) *BBC admits Iraq scoop was flawed.* The Times, August 13th; p. 1.

Webster, P. (2003) *Adviser wanted 'a win not a draw' in BBC battle.* The Times, September 23rd; p. 1.

Webster, P. and D. Charter. (2003) *Campbell accuses BBC of lying.* The Times, June 26th; p. 1.

Webster, P., D. Charter, T. Baldwin and R. Bennett. (2003) *Labour MPs told to blitz the BBC.* The Times, June 28th; p. 1.

Webster, P. and D. Charter. (2003) *Blair's defiance leaves Labour critics unmoved.* The Times, July 17th; p. 10.

Webster, P. and D. Charter. (2003) *Blair's defiance leaves Labour critics unmoved.* The Times, July 17th; p. 10.

Webster, P. and R. Snoddy. (2003) *BBC in crisis as Blair mood swings.* The Times, July 21st; p. 1.

The Times. 2003. *'Mr Campbell should withdraw claims of bias'.* July 7th; p. 8.
The Times. 2003. *A report that leaves key question unanswered.* July 8th; p. 19.
The Times. 2003. *The danger of doubt.* July 28th; p. 17.
The Times. 2003. *Alastair Campbell under fire in Court 73.* August 20th; p. 1.
The Times. 2003. *Blair's tribute: 'Loyal, able and fearless'.* August 30th; p. 5.
The Times. 2003. *Media cynicism killing politics, Campbell says.* November 26th; p. 2.

WEBSITES

The Hutton Inquiry Website - http://webarchive.nationalarchives.gov.uk/20090128221546/http://www.the-hutton-inquiry.org.uk/ (23/02/2012).
The White House President George Bush. President Bush Delivers Graduation Speech at West Point – http://georgewbush-whitehouse.archives.gov/news/releases/2002/06/print/20020601-3.html (21/03/2012).
House of Commons, Foreign Affairs Committee. 2003. The Decision to go to War in Iraq. Ninth Report of Session 2002–03. http://www.fas.org/irp/threat/ukiraq0703.pdf (14/03/2012).

"If you do not believe it just ask them". The credibility management of the Catholic Church in the 8x1000 campaigns

Paolo Peverini

INTRODUCTION

The issue of credibility plays a very important role in the semiotic theory. As Greimas and Courtés (2007) have remarked, Saussure's theory, postulating the autonomy and the inherent character of each language and, at the same time, the impossibility of using an external referent, has pushed the semiotic to shift its attention from the problem of the 'truth' to the problem of the 'narrative of truth': the *veridiction*. In this perspective, the credibility of a discourse and of its interlocutors is conceived as the result of a tricky process, a *contract of veridiction* responding to multiple and complex logics.

The truthfulness of a message, in a semiotic perspective, is conceived as a meaning effect, as the constantly renegotiable product of inner mechanisms of a text through which an enunciator proposes to an enunciatee a speech that appears "true", "impartial", "transparent".

In a media landscape thoroughly permeated by the complex logics of the seeming *true*, the concept of 'veridiction' and its mechanisms within texts, different for languages, genres and formats, can be useful to critically analyze the strategic decisions carried out by a subject damaged by rumors (Fabbri, Pezzini, 1998; Livolsi, Volli, 2005) or by documented scandals in order to re-negotiate the credibility of his intentions, the "truth" of his message.

Following the theoretical and methodological approach of semiotics, it can be useful to focus attention on the enunciative strategic rearrangement prompted by the discourses that affect the credibility of a public subject and by the revelations that openly criticize the consistency among the set of values that define his identity and his actions in a social context.

Accordingly, a very interesting discursive "place" is social communication, which represents a media field heavily stressed by several problematic elements that constantly force a large number of subjects of enunciation to reconfigure the forms of their own discourse, problematizing the truth of their statements. As Nicoletta Bosco states (2011, p. 25), at the opening of the Second Report on the Social Communication in Italy:

> Besides the economic aspects, further elements of crisis crossed the Italian society: a complex set of events, with many consequences, including judicial ones, has uncovered widespread corruption and collusion between politics and crime, but also sex scandals and episodes of pedophilia. They are phenomena that, although of different nature, have involved important actors of the italian political and public scene, and even senior echelons of the Catholic Church, not only in our country. All these circumstances fostered a gradual contraction of public economic resources earmarked for the execution of services and interventions for citizens and communities, included the symbolic ones, such as trust in institutions.

The wide scope of social communication, marked by the presence of subjects different for objectives, issues addressed, organization of means and modes of their exercise, is an ideal discursive field to make a reflection on the strategies that move the communicative action of individuals forced to constantly renegotiate their legitimacy with the public opinion.

Within this field with uncertain boundaries and affected by constant change, an interesting area is represented by the social advertising, a key element in the effectiveness of fund-raising activities, which are essential to ensure the survival of several subjects. As is intuitive, the social advertising is a field marked by a fierce competition in order to gain financial support, and the many subjects that manage its languages and contents challenge with the implicit aim of strengthening the link between social engagement that they promote and their own visual identity (Floch, 1997). At the same time, the social advertising has an essential feature that distinguishes it from the commercial advertising, with which, however, it shares many features (Volli, 2005): that is the impossibility for any subject of enunciation to openly claim a position of strength compared to its counterparts (civil society, donors, competitors). On the background of the values that affect the content of social advertising, the competition between the various players of the communication often looks like a silent and indirect[1] comparison for the acquisition of credibility and support from the taxpayers.

The use by a growing number of people to the language of advertising as a communication resource to mobilize support makes the set of discourses concerning the

---

1 There are some exceptions, e.g. the communication methods adopted by UAAR, the Union of Rationalist Atheists and Agnostics.

fund-raising an exemplary discursive field, whose analysis is useful to answer some questions. As mentioned, this intrinsically dynamic scenario, in recent years has been marked by several crises of legitimacy sometimes particularly intense. What happens when the truth of a social message is "contended" among different parties that seek the financial support to operate? How can be translated in terms of communication strategy the crisis of legitimacy affecting certain actors involved in the field of solidarity? What backlashes and adjustments are arranged by an enunciator to reinforce and renegotiate the contract of veridiction that binds him to his deceived audience?

In order to articulate a reflection on undoubtedly complex and far-reaching issues, it may be useful to limit the scope of investigation, trying to isolate a field particularly representative of some general mechanisms. In this regard, the Italian institute of the of 8x1000 represents a discursive sphere functional to highlight some questions that can be useful to mention. As Lo Chirco (2008, p. 1-2) points out:

> With the 8x1000 advertising, the discourse of religion is pointed out in an advertising perspective, representing a kind of interreligious dialogue sui generis. The churches/communities behave like real brands, competing for the signatures and attention of believer "taxpayers" (or taxpayers "believers") [...] it costs nothing, and moreover it is useful to help people: this is the real difference with the classic brand advertising. In this regard, the wishes of the citizens (who normally consider a right duty being helpful for other people) are embodied by the enunciator-Church. It can be compared to the category of "institutional advertising": this kind of advertising outlines a company's image as a whole, trying to change the perception of consumers[...] It covers the same places of traditional advertising: the block of commercials that interrupts the viewing of a movie or the listening to the radio, or among the pages of a magazine, between an article about politics and another about trends.

In particular, the transformations that have marked over the years the use of the language and techniques of advertising by the Catholic Church are strongly characterized not only, of course, by the thematization of credibility, but by the problematization of its *mise-en-scène* as a value. In other words, as the analysis of the social advertising texts will point out, over the time the critics of the 8x1000 tool and its use by the Catholic Church, the scandals that have strongly called into question her credibility have played a key role in changing the advertising strategy, helping to radically replace the content and the style of discourse. The criticism towards the Catholic Church's credibility and legitimacy in the employment of financial resources gathered through the 8x1000 are reflected in her own language, as it's clearly shown by the slogan that accompanies the last complex and wide inter media communication campaign, which will be discussed in the following paragraphs: "If you do not believe it, just ask them".

As Giampaolo Fabris (1995, p. 587) observes, the widespread skepticism that has for long been associated with the expression *non-profit advertising* reveals to be completely unfounded since the alleged opposition between consumer and citizen, or between consumer and individual is completely artificial.

> Although the advertising aimed at collective purposes has an "ancient heart", and its current practice has many antecedents, only in recent decades it is beginning to emerge. And it is even in more recent times that its spread is remarkable. In recent years, the struggle against terrible diseases, civic education, fund raising for humanitarian purposes, the promotion of public services seem to find a formidable ally in advertising.

As underlined by Dario E. Viganò (2011), among the various texts of the advertising language, within the 8x1000 field, the commercial has marked since the beginning the communicative action of the Church which has always practiced the strategy of virtuous behavior.
As Manetti points out (2006, pp. 8-9).

> The social advertising can alternately lean on one of two opposing strategies. The first is provoking, showing the negative effects of a certain socially reprehensible behavior [...] The other strategy instead consists in showing a good behavior, proposing it as a model to imitate, or, on the contrary, calls to abandon such negative behaviors as, for example, among the many that affect our not always so progressed civilization, the intolerance towards people of other cultures, the lack of sensitivity towards handicap, etc..

As Viganò remarks (2011, p. 91), the effort that from the beginning has marked the planning of communication campaigns of the CEI (Italian Episcopal Community).

> [...] Was, therefore, to conceive a format made up of a "fixed" frame which is easily recognizable and connected to the 8x1000 campaign and to the values of the Catholic Church, upon which different stories are set, able to restore the complexity of actions in which the Church is committed and which are made possible thanks to the 8x1000 contributions; a television campaign with a "multi-subject" nature (six or seven 30-second spot), composed of stories to be aired in rotation over five months.

These initial considerations clearly show the strategic and at the same time highly problematic role that is given to the audiovisual form of the commercial in the overall communication strategy of the Church, a textual form that contains a double function: informational and promotional.
On the one hand, indeed, the spots respond to the primary need of informing taxpayers about the mechanism of the 8x1000 and about the destination of funds, on the other hand they are functional to the promotion of the founding values of the Catholic religion and try to reassert the Church's credibility. As we will see, in a

diachronic perspective, the commercials created for the 8x1000 campaigns underline continuous transformations of the communicative contract between enunciators and enunciatees, an enunciative relationship that the semiotic theory outlines as a proposal of meaning that necessarily undergoes constant adjustments, connected to the changeable margin of credibility of the players involved.

> A communicative contract is not stipulated: rather it is re-stipulated, it is reaffirmed or it is modified, charged with new meaning and values, starting from socio-communicative situations [...] or more or less contingent marketing, political, cultural circumstances (Marrone, 2007, p. 164).

Before focusing on the single textual forms that concern the communicative strategy of the 8x1000, we must underline that the critical issues in the use of advertising messages by the Catholic Church must be framed within a broader discourse that regards the use of social advertising as a lever of the fund-raising processes. In this perspective, it is not possible to delve into the management of communication initiatives concerning credibility, carried out by the Church, without considering, even briefly, the important issue of some specific features that characterize the category of social advertising, with particular attention to the crucial stage of fund-raising. This type of communication campaigns features the solicitation of a pathemic involvement by the audience, the ability of subjects of the enunciation, that play within a strongly competitive framework, to hold and manage the logic of affects and collective passions on each textual level (narrative, enunciative, figurative). The pathemic dimension, on which the whole discursive organization is based, and on which we measure the communication strategies of all actors involved, is undoubtedly the *solidarity* that is inscribed into texts by using a variety of themes, narrative configurations and more or less codified figures, recognizable by audiences and donors.

As remarked by Popescu-Jourdy in an essay specifically dedicated to the communicative logics and practices involved in social communication campaigns, the etymology of the word *solidarity* refers to a legal principle (*in solidum*) that recognizes the mutual accountability among different actors regarding a common debt:

> Dans le Code de Justinien, le mot latin solidus se rapporte à l'interdépendance des débiteurs entre eux. Chacun est engagé, en termes de dette et de responsabilité, pour le tout (*in solidum*). Le concept - qui rejoint sans doute l'idée pythagoricienne du nombre - insiste sur une totalité, une unité dont la sollicitude s'exerce sur chaque être qui la constitue. *In solidum* reconnaît donc la responsabilité solidaire entre plusieurs acteurs pour une dette reconnue et considérée comme étant commune (...) Stratégies de développement, de ressources humaines ou de gestion financière constituent désormais le quotidien des organisations comme Handicap International, la Croix Rouge ou l'UNICEF. Ainsi, à leur tour, les organisations

de ce type renforcent l'image sociale de la solidarité et imposent des formes institutionelles de l'action solidaire (Popescu-Jourdy, 2011, pp. 577-579).

As the value of solidarity is the foundation of the *fiduciary contract* sought in any advertising text that underlies the discourse of fund-raising, (regardless of the identity of the promoter, of his objectives, his program), the crucial issue of the credibility of the promoting subject may be revisited in relation to the capacity of the enunciator to strategically manage several stereotypes that strongly influence the effectiveness of the "dialogue" with the donor.

Stereotypes of social advertising should not be intended only on a visual level, as figures of a more or less limited repertoire of images related to the theme of a campaign, but also on the narrative level (stories of solidarity) and on the pathemic dimension. In particular, in social advertising it is possible to find, as indeed commonly happens in commercial advertising too, a whole repertoire of "typical characters that presents such quite predictable affective virtues, as to become the representatives par excellence of a particular passion"(Marrone, 2007, p. 132). For instance, we can mention the codified representations that give shape in fund-raising campaigns to the pathemic roles of the *rancorous*, the *diffident* and the *altruist*. The widespread use of stereotypes and the speed with which the alternative strategies of social communication, typical of the unconventional marketing (Peverini, 2009, 2011), are assimilated and re-proposed, inevitably affect the effectiveness of social advertising, a field whose strength on the pragmatic level collides with the codified images of the *aestheticization of* suffering (Boltanski, 2000), with the media representations of the *"pain of others"* (Sontag, 2006).

8X1000 AND TV COMMERCIALS. THE CREDIBILITY OF THE CATHOLIC CHURCH AND THE CHALLENGE OF FUND-RAISING

The 8x1000 advertising strategy is declined in several commercials that cover a period of over twenty years (since 1990), representing a textual corpus of great interest for a sociosemiotic analysis that aims at reading texts in search of traces of a constant re-negotiation of a credibility often openly criticized. In this section, the attention will focus on various important aspects in the management and treatment of credibility by the enunciator. The textual analysis of the 8x1000 campaigns of the Catholic Church allows to point out some significant changes in communication tactics, not mere transformations on the surface, but overall re-corrections that affect the language used to search for and encourage the solidarity of taxpayers on several levels. The aim of the analysis of the 8x1000 advertising materials is not therefore to retrace the history of social communication campaigns[2]; rather, we will question the way in which the scandals that have affected the credibility of the Catholic Church gradually gained importance in texts up to significantly influence the choice of the thematic isotopy around which the current inter media communication plan has been designed.

A first basic consideration concerns the progressively more aware use of television and of the form of commercials by the Church. In the starting phase of the 8x1000 campaigns, the necessity to provide informations on the new instrument prevails, the narrative style is pedagogical, played by the institutional voice of an extradiegetic narrator who addresses the audience using the strategy of *"call for solidarity"*, as it is clearly proved by two slogans used between 1990 and 1994: "Without your help we can not do miracles, " It costs you nothing, but the Italian Catholic Church can do so much".

On the figurative level, the expressive choices are very simple, very far from the sleek visual style, so widely diffused in television advertising. A first important difference comes out in 1994, when a marked narrativization of the theme of solidarity emerges. In a spot entitled "The Bell", the roles of the instance of enunciation (the Church) and of the enunciatee (the believers/taxpayers) are for the first time represented, respectively, by a priest and by the small community of his parish church. The driving purpose of this campaign is declining in a more articulated form the fiduciary contract, setting up a story expressly based on a metaphor. The sharing of resources and responsibilities, that contributes to define the message of solidarity in all the 8x1000 campaigns, is here proposed for the first time in a narrative way: the paradigmatic history of a joint effort necessary to hoist a heavy bell on top of the parish church becomes a symbol of the cooperation pact between the Church and the believers.

The narrator's voice once again is external and has a double function: on one side it shows the employment of the financial resources obtained with the support of taxpayers, on the other it outlines the actors' narrative programs, helping to shape, through an acting that emphatically stresses the euphoric atmosphere of the story, the strategy of emotional involvement that defines the message and that reaches its climax in the final enthusiastic reaction of the community.

Significantly, in this first phase, we assist to a marked fictionalization of the social discourse. In the euphemistic communication strategy there is no space for the dysphoric passions of social advertising, the main expressive elements of the audiovisual text (direction, photography, sound track, extradiegetic narrator's voice) make the promotional nature of the message clear. In this phase, the requests of solidarity and

---

[2] As for this topic, see the work of Dario Edoardo Viganò (2011).

economic support are not yet associated, within the text, to the crucial issue of the Church credibility.

On this side, the following years marked a significant reversal. The slogan chosen to open the campaign "Where does the 8x1000 Irpef tax assigned to the Catholic Church go?" faces two critical needs: reaffirming the fiduciary contract with the believers and, at the same time, rewriting its fundamentals. On a general communication strategy, there is the effort to fill the gap with the public taxpayers, forgoing the sleek commercials in favor of a greater realistic effect, and to express in a more articulate terms the theme of solidarity. In particular, the need of arguing the enunciator's commitment is inscribed into the text, highlighting the outcomes achieved with the support of the believers. Significantly, for the first time, the campaign emphasizes the delicate issue of the credibility of Catholic Church solidarity made possible by 8x1000; it becomes the main thematic isotopy of a discourse whose purpose is to give the spectator the impression of the utmost transparency on ethical level, particularly concerning the use of financial resources.

In terms of enunciation, the doubt about the Church's social action (expressed in the form of a question addressed to taxpayers and believers) is used to frame the enunciator's discourse, in order to reformulate his request for credibility, and introduce the spectator to a series of micro stories focused on several key topics such as job placement, **rehabilitation**, restauration, etc. Thus, the communication campaigns plan is made up of thematic chapters presented in the form of life stories, fragments of experiences told as paradigmatic practices of active engagement. An emblematic example of this strategy is the commercial dedicated to care services that, on the visual lever, answers the question "Where does the 8x1000 Irpef tax assigned to the Catholic Church go?" through an handheld close-up shot of a nun engaged in moving a heavy pot on the stove of a busy kitchen. The religious who appear in the audiovisual text are framed during daily tasks, filmed in action inside a space at the same time real and invested with a symbolic value: a shelter for the homeless in Rome. The story of solidarity is not entrusted only to priests and nuns but also to young volunteers engaged in every day work: in this case a young woman answers the question of the enunciator: "Here, look: they are all homeless, but here they have found much more than a roof".

The differences with the first phase of the 8x1000 campaigns are evident, especially as regards the effort to distinguish itself from the style of commercial advertising. In particular, it is interesting to underline how in this case the presence of the enunciator is articulated on two levels: the voice-over and the character. Generally, in the forms of commercial advertising centered on the logic of argumentation, the discourse is assigned either to a character or to a narrative instance that is anonymous and omniscient; in these spots, however, the enunciation adopts a double register with the explicit objective of reaffirming the "long-distance dialogue" with its interlocutors, seeking the trust of its supporters and responding to the distrust and criticism of many detractors.

In this sense, the style of acting of the voice-over is completely reconsidered too: the participatory emphasis of the narrator is abandoned in favor of a softer style, the grain of the voice, which always plays a crucial role in building meaning effects in the advertising discourse, here becomes a tool within a strategy that aims at emotionally involve the spectator. As Vanoye and Goliot-Leté (1998, p. 122) recall, the voice:

> Overarches the images, it gives them a sense (the phenomenon of rooting) in some way, but often it goes beyond what the image shows. Observe, listen to some spots containing a voice-over: you will find that the comment, is it argumentative, explicative, pushing, "exceeds" a lot the image. In addition, the voice carries its own potential of purely sound seduction with its own tonality and grain.

The explicitation of the issue of credibility and its narrativization continues in the subsequent years: in particular, a significant date in the rearrangement of the fiduciary relationship between the Church and the believer is 1999, when the new communication campaign is built on a series of life stories and the position of the narrator is deeply revised in order to strengthen the overall credibility of the religious discourse. The narrative voice, so far carried out by an instance external to the story, (a voice of support for images with a clear educational goal), is now placed in the text and explicitly invested with a very strong symbolic value: reiterating the relationship between the evangelical word and the call for support, which is an aspect very often called into question by scandals that affect the credibility of the Church.

In this campaign, the narrator does not simply play a role of counterpoint to the images, but he is also a guidance for the interpretation of the story. The narrator becomes a figure that calls firsthand the believer, acting, as it happens in the spot entitled "Operas", as an element of connection between God and the human community: "I was thirsty and you gave me drink, I was in prison and you came to me, I was a stranger and you welcomed me. Whenever you did it to one of these my brethren, ye have done it unto me".

On the visual level, the choice of images reflects the need to expand the fundamental theme of solidarity. Famine, detention, loneliness are subjects of short stories set up according to a recursive framework based on two moments: a first step that shows the disease and the request for support, a second step dedicated to the positive sanction of the problem, made possible by the solidarity of the people.

Furthermore, in this period the pathemic dimension assumes an increasingly decisive role in the building of audiovisual narrations, anticipating a feature that in the subsequent years will mark all the 8x1000 campaigns. In this regard, it should be noted that in a semiotic perspective, in every form of discourse, not only in advertising, passion involves two levels, distinct and, at the same time, in relation to each other: the level of the enunciate and the level of enunciation. On the first side, the passion is intended as the object of the discourse, as a content explained, the "what" mentioned in the text. In the field of social advertising, this issue concerns passions showed in the single commercials and in the communication campaign as a whole: suffering, joy, hope, for instance, constitute a very important part of the contents conveyed by the Church, represented through a "repertoire" of more or less codified forms. In the advertising production of this period, in particular, solidarity explicitly appears in the gesture of a priest who places his hand on the shoulder of a prisoner, while happiness is represented through the smile of a nun who is holding a baby in a pediatric hospital, looking directly at the camera.

Regarding the enunciation, otherwise, passion does not relate to the audiovisual content but to the form of its discourse; in other words, it concerns the role that film direction and editing play in the overall ability of the text to solicit the pathemic involvement of the viewer. Therefore, in the first case we refer to the discourse of passion, in the second we refer to the passionate discourse.

As for this latter point, if we look back at the commercials included in the 8x1000 campaign in 1999, we can underline that the choices regarding the soundtrack play a key role in building the effectiveness of the discourse in terms of pathemic involvement. Accordingly, it is important to underline how in social advertising the music is inevitably entrusted with a series of connotative meanings that provide indications about the urgency of the issue, the identity of the enunciator and his aims. Hence, the expressive choices defining the entire production of Catholic Church communication campaigns belong to the strategy of euphemism. In the "Operas" adv, in particular, the soundtrack clearly works as a musical counterpoint to the religious discourse, it is an essential component of its pathemic effectiveness. The images of solidarity, on the background provided by the sound of the flute, the regular rhythm, the melody of the song, are invested with a sentimental and positive value, they reactivate several stereotypes about the passion, especially hope that, as Alessandro Melchiorri (2002, p. 118) remarks, always plays a key role in the communication strategy of the social advertising.

> Passions that look at the future, such as hope, are typical of social advertising campaigns: aid to third world countries, fight against incurable disease. It is hard to find out passions that look at the past. The apparently dysphoric connotation of a passion as nostalgia makes problematic its presence in advertising. The nostalgic subject is in a state of disjunction from its object, and remembers the time when it was tied to it. Because the nostalgia appears in the advertising message it is necessary that the reunion with the object seems at least possible.

In commercials that belong to this phase of the communicative action of the Church, hope concerns not only the content level, but the overall expression plane of the text; the protagonists of the actions of solidarity, religious and laymen, operate closely together, they are always committed on the territory, undertaking simple and everyday tasks. The camera is always focused on the confident expressions of the subjects, the search for a contact with the enunciatee is stressed, in terms of expression, with the frequent use of the look at the camera that inscribes into the text the aim to emphasize the double demand for support and trust.

The role of the pathemic dimension in the effectiveness of advertising discourse is even more explicit in the communication campaign of the year 2000, where the choice to reaffirm the strong joint between the values of the catholic religion and the request for financial support is translated into the decision to entrust the instance of enunciation of the text to Gospel: "For two thousand years the words of Gospel offered comfort, hope and courage". The passional dimension of discourse permeates this slogan that closes the series of commercials dedicated to the theme of maternal love or to the parable of the lost sheep; these are two emblematic cases of rhetoric of collective passions used by the enunciator in order to reassert his credibility, the legitimacy of his discourse and his demands to the believers.

An interesting aspect to point out is the presence in these audiovisual texts of young men and women who reenact the events narrated in the Gospel by replacing the characters of religious in the realization of narrative programs that define the advertising discourse of the Church. The images of young people who assist the needy play, obviously, a strategic role in the awareness action of the Church: the request for support firstly enhancing not the institution and its direct representative, but rather the specific commitment in the social field, the urgency of the solidarity.

"IF YOU DO NOT BELIEVE IT JUST ASK THEM"

Over the years, the criticism towards the Church, with particular reference to the use of financial resources obtained through the 8x1000 campaigns, have made the issue of her credibility increasingly crucial, up to the "If you do not believe it just ask them" inter media campaign that has been completely built around this theme. Currently the aim of the communicative actions carried out by C.E.I. is explicitly based on the need to reiterate transparency in the management of funds; this goal is expressed through a semiotic strategy conceived by the enunciator in order to show to taxpayers and believers the effect of maximum transparency and honesty in his activity. In the media environment, where the discourse of solidarity takes shape, the form of the commercial is obviously still present; however it is only a part of a much wider "dialogue" in which advertising and information are combined in complex ways.

A first important consideration concerns the structured and not episodic nature of the communication project. A website[3] has been conceived as the institutional "media place" where all the informations and initiatives related to the 8x1000 campaign converge. Significantly, in the home page the issue of transparency is explicitly emphasized. Along with an interactive and constantly updated map of Italy, the user is encouraged to browse through the initiatives carried out thanks to funding received, while a synthetic text illustrates C.E.I.'s intention to reassert its commitment in terms of transparency[4]. The site map is divided into a number of pages reserved to the "financial statement", to "how to sign", to "Initiatives", to the "documentary", to the "YouTube channel". A second website[5], connected to the first one and specifically dedicated to the campaign "If you do not believe it just ask them", is very interesting in the context of a semiotic reflection about communication response to the crisis of credibility. This initiative, clearly aimed to reaffirm the authenticity of the Church commitment in the social field, is once again centered around a set of life stories, but, at the same time, it introduces some new elements compared to the previously analyzed campaigns. In an enunciative perspective, the story is divided into several discursive frames nested into each other, in order to obtain a realistic effect.

---

3 www.8x1000.it
4 Here's the text: "C.E.I. is committed in a "transparency project" that goes beyond legal duties about the annual 8x1000 to the Catholic Church annual report (art. 44, 222/85) [...] The 8x1000 map is an interactive tool that allows to visualize and localize the initiatives funded by C.E.I. on the national territory. Informations are constantly updated, because every diocese, that locally manages funds, is able to upload on the map its own financial statement. It is a unique and innovative transparency project that shows on a map thousands of interventions.
5 http://www.chiediloaloro.it/

http://www.chiediloaloro.it/

Firstly, the Catholic Church, as the enunciator of the campaign, tries to reiterate the credibility of her discourse by delegating the narration to eight bloggers, that are the protagonists of a diary divided into episodes and presented as the real documentation of the projects realized with the 8x1000 funding: "They are not reporters, or journalists. They are 8 people like you. They're touring Italy to tell about the 8x1000 works. This is their diary. "

Within this strategy, designed to produce the maximum grade of objectivization, the eight narrators delegate the narration of the solidarity to the protagonists of the projects financed by C.E.I. on the italian territory.

The choice of the diary form, the emphasis on the non-professionalism of the bloggers involved in first person to document the use of funds by the Catholic Church, the possibility for the user to be constantly updated on the steps of the eight reporters journey are clear signs of a communication strategy that aims to reduce the distance between the addresser and the addressee of the discourse and, at the same time, to look for the last one's confidence.

The enunciator claims his credibility, in a more marked manner, the more explicit is the awareness about criticisms received. In this sense, the fiduciary contract with the enunciatee is reconfigured by delegating the discourse to an intermediate figure,

http://www.chiediloaloro.it/

the blogger-volunteer; he clearly plays the thematic role of the witness, mediating on the narrative and enunciative levels, between the institution of the Church and her representatives on the territory: religious and laymen.

Looking at the campaigns in a diachronic perspective, it is possible to observe how the visual and narrative point of view progressively shifted from an external instance to a character inside the story. This rearrangement coincides within the text with the mise en scène of the proposal for a new fiduciary contract between enunciator and enunciatee, no longer based on a explicit pedagogical relation, but on an apparently equal relationship, in which the believer, seen as a potential supporter of the Church, is portrayed as the bearer of a doubt that is shared and rooted in the community.

In this regard, the slogan, that marks the website and all the communication materials, has the duty to reverse the distrust into trust, not only explicitly thematizing the theme of the doubt, but rather expressing it in a very refined manner. Firstly, the phrase "If you do not believe it just ask them" is characterized by an evident polysemy;

the direct interpellation addressed to the addressee leads to a plurality of meanings. "If you do not believe it" can express the diffidence towards the institution of the Catholic Church, towards the works realized with the financial support of the 8x1000 or, of course, towards the religion itself. On the latter point, in particular, we should remark a deviation from the slogans and, more generally, from the communication strategies of the previous campaigns. For the first time, indeed, the enunciator openly addresses not only to taxpayers, but to the entire community, to believers, to atheists and to agnostics. In this perspective, the slogan clearly refers to the strong criticisms raised against the use of Church funds by such groups as the UAAR, the Union of Rationalist Atheists and Agnostics.

The second part of the slogan, "just ask them" implicates the presence in the discourse of three different subjects involved in the story of solidarity: the bloggers, the operators on the territory committed in the implementation of the projects financed with funds from the 8x1000 campaign and, obviously, the needy.

Each of these subjects has its own textual space on the website, which, is, once again, clearly focused on several life stories. The discursive style employed in the clips is homogeneous and it aims at reiterating the effect of the maximum realism of the stories (use of hand-held camera, no soundtrack, real life noise). Moreover, each documented experience is introduced by a short clip where the voice-over of an "institutional" narra-

UAAR, the Union of Rationalist Atheists and Agnostics

tor presents the scenario in which the initiative of support takes shape, briefly describing the problems to be solved, the solutions adopted and the profile of the actors involved.

In conclusion, the communication project of the Catholic Church appears to have progressively been concentrated around a *strategy of transparency* that clearly represents the communicative response to the crisis of credibility of the institution. An entire section of the website is significantly dedicated to this theme with the so-called "White Book" project, which is an informative, yet promotional initiative dedicated to reiterate the proposal of a new fiduciary contract with the community of supporters. An agreement subject to constant, inevitable renegotiations.

> The signature for the destination of the 8xt1000 to the Catholic Church is not an abstract action, but it is something that reaches every corner of our country. The south, north, center, far away or just around your home. The White Book is a project for transparency proposed and coordinated by the Service for the promotion of the economic support to the Catholic Church in partnership with 226 Italian dioceses and other offices and services of the C.E.I. - Italian Episcopal Conference. The White Book website gives the opportunity to interactively explore the funds we have received, when and how they were used, what works, but also to know the thousand faces of the priests and their silent engagement that offers to many people the chance of a better life.
>
> The White Book is a project for transparency in constant update and evolution that involves a lot of data and informations, therefore not limited to the use of the 8x1000 funds on the territory. The C.E.I. does not entirely fund the work for educational and ecclesiastics principles. It is believed that the cooperation of the local organizations is an expression of participation and shared responsibility. The C.E.I., therefore, operates with a maximum contribution of 75% of the budgeted expenditure.

UAAR, the Union of Rationalist Atheists and Agnostics

REFERENCES

Boltanski L. (2000), *Lo spettacolo del dolore*, Raffaello Cortina, Milano (ed. or. *La souffrance à distance. Morale humanitaire, médias et politique*, Métailié, Paris 1993).

Bosco, N. (a cura di) (2011), *Secondo rapporto sulla comunicazione sociale in Italia*, Carocci, Roma.

Centro TraMe (2011) *La forma e l'impronta del dolore. Percorsi nella fotografia della sofferenza*, in E|C serie speciale, nn. 7-8, pp. 158-177.

Fabbri P. Pezzini I. (a cura di) (1998), *Voci e rumori: la propagazione della parola*, in Versus. Quaderni di studi semiotici, 79.

Fabris G. (1995), *La pubblicità. Teorie e prassi*, FrancoAngeli, Milano.

Floch J.M. (1992), *Semiotica, marketing, comunicazione*, FrancoAngeli, Milano (ed. or. *Sémiotique, marketing et communication*, PUF, Paris 1990).

Floch J.M. (1997), *Identità visive*, FrancoAngeli, Milano (ed. or. *Identités visuelles*, PUF, Paris 1995).

Gabardi E. (a cura di) (2011), *Social Advertising. Campagne pubblicitarie per un mondo migliore*, FrancoAngeli, Milano.

Gadotti G., Bernocchi R. (2010), *La pubblicità sociale. Maneggiare con cura*, Carocci, Roma.

Greimas A.J., Courtés J. (2007), *Semiotica. Dizionario ragionato della teoria del linguaggio*, Mondadori, Milano (ed. or. *Sémiotique. Dictionnaire raisonné de la théorie du langage*, Hachette, Paris 1979).

Livolsi M., Volli U. (a cura di) (2005), *Rumor e pettegolezzi. L'importanza della comunicazione informale*, FrancoAngeli, Milano.

Lo Chirco M. (2008), *Il discorso delle religioni intorno all'otto per mille*, in E|C (www.ec-aiss.it).

Manetti G. (2006), *Specchio delle mie brame. Dodici anni di spot televisivi*, Ets, Pisa.

Marrone G. (2007). *Il discorso di marca. Modelli semiotici per il branding*, Laterza, Roma-Bari.

Melchiorri A. (2002), "La dimensione patemica negli spot", in Pezzini I. (a cura di), *Trailer, spot, clip, siti, banner. Le forme brevi della comunicazione audiovisiva*, Meltemi, Roma, pp. 111-146.

Peverini P., Spalletta M. (2009), *Unconventional. Valori, testi, pratiche della pubblicità sociale*, Meltemi, Roma.

Peverini P. (2011), "Il visibile non convenzionale. Strategie del social guerrilla", in Migliore T., (a cura di) *Retorica del visibile. Strategie dell'immagine tra significazione e comunicazione*, Roma, Aracne, pp. 632-644.

Pezzini I. (a cura di) (2002), *Trailer, spot, clip, siti, banner. Le forme brevi della comunicazione audiovisiva*, Meltemi, Roma.

Popescu-Jourdy, D. (2011) "L'image humanitaire: dispositifs et pratiques de communication", in Migliore T., (a cura di) *Retorica del visibile. Strategie dell'immagine tra significazione e comunicazione*, Roma, Aracne, pp. 577-588.

Sontag, S. (2006), *Davanti al dolore degli altri*, Mondadori, Milano (ed. or. *Regarding the pain of others*, Farrar, Straus and Giroux, New York 2003).

Vanoye F., Goliot-Lété A. (1998), *Introduzione all'analisi del film*, Lindau, Torino (ed. or. Précis d'analyse filmique, Nathan, Paris 1992).

Viganò D.E. (2011), *Chiesa e pubblicità. Storia e analisi degli spot 8x1000*, Rubbettino, Soveria-Mannelli.

Volli U. (2005), *Laboratorio di semiotica*, Laterza, Roma-Bari.

The construction of credibility: a case study from television

Donatella Selva

It is worth to analyze the case of the Italian TV show *Serviziopubblico* (literally, "public service") in terms of communication and promotional strategy because it has been an experiment of synthesis of mainstream and usual ingredients with an alternative way of broadcasting and a resistant approach. These two last elements are in particular the key points upon which the promotional campaign has been focused: *Serviziopubblico* wanted the public to recognize its value of counter-information service on public's behalf. It is an excellent case study for the process of "competition for credibility" that Gili noticed as increasing in contemporary Italian context, parallel with the processes of mediatization and personalization of the political struggle (Gili, 2010; Sorice, 2011):

> "In relation with the increasing political struggle, as it happened in Italy during last decades, some media, plainly lined up for diverse political forces, engage a daily fight aimed to discredit the opposite party leaders, but also harshly debate against media and journalist who join it, accusing each other for being professional faker and "hack" on the pay roll of one or another leader, party or trend" (Gili, 2010, p. 41).

INTRODUCTION

Serviziopubblico started on November 3rd 2011 and is still broadcast every Thursday in prime time. It is a political talk show, where relevant political and social issues are debated by politicians, critics, journalists. A small group of representatives of common people and associations are invited to talk about the subject of the episode because of being somehow involved in it: for example, workers from an industry which is closing due to the economic crisis, students protesting against the university bill of reform, citizens exhausted by politicians' privileges.

The structure of the program consist in the anchorman, the journalist Michele Santoro, opening each episode with a two-up-to-fiveminutes monologue, in which he launches the issue of the day and comments it according his own opinion. For example, on March 22nd 2012, he introduces the theme of corruption with those words:

> "But, no matter which your opinion about it could be, let's pretend that the first thing to do to modernize our country would be an immediate reduction of pensions. Let's pretend that the second one would be to make easier [for employers] to fire us all immediately. But is there someone who can explain me which is the reason why they don't put the same force, the same energy, and above all, the same urgency, in fighting against tax evasion and corruption?".[1]

Although it is just one extract, it is a perfect example of Santoro's typical way of hosting. In effect he plays the role of a member of the common people, who is subjected to the government's decisions as much as every citizen is. A common citizen who thinks Mario Monti's government is iniquitous when trying to solve the economic crisis through reforming welfare and labour market rules, instead of focusing on money waste, corruption, and privileges of leading classes.

At the same time, he cannot fully succeed in merge with its public because of his well-known reputation of professional and his recent past of European Parliament member. It can be useful to briefly trace his story to fully understand the show genesis.

Then we are going to analyze three particular moments in which the host speaks to his public: first, when he is going to host the last episode of his show in Rai; second, when he ask for crowdfounding; third, opening the first episode of his new show. As we will see, those speeches are fundamental stages for the construction of the show's credibility.

AN EPIC STRUGGLE

Michele Santoro has always been closer to a showman and a host than to an impartial, objective journalist:

> "The media historian Peppino Ortoleva described him in an interview with the present author as an integral member of a television oligarchy, which practiced a journalism that was politically biased and characterized by 'improvisation and demagogy with the tendency to judge and not to inform" (Rothenberg, 2009, p. 219).

---

1 http://www.serviziopubblico.it/articolo/dettaglio/479/page/1.

Since 1982 in Rai, he has been hosting many TV shows, in particular political talk shows since 1987, with a parenthesis of eight years in Mediaset. The formula of his shows has always been quite the same: political and social issues were discussed with attention to the "voice of common people", interviewed in its "natural" setting (industries, streets, schools) or through a small group of representatives in studio.[2]

The relationship between Santoro and Rai begins to be troubled in 2002, when Santoro was fired due to the opposition of the Prime Minister Silvio Berlusconi and his right-wing coalition. The episode of the Santoro's dismissal is subsequent to the so-called "Bulgarian Diktat" pronounced by Berlusconi during an official visit in Sofia, Bulgaria, when he addressed to Santoro and other two Rai hosts, the journalist Enzo Biagi and the comedian Daniele Luttazzi, accusing them of "using public television in a criminal manner".[3] Since Rai's executive board is nominated by a Parliament Committee and the Ministry of Economy, it is deeply connected with the Parliamentarian majority and the government: this has influenced the management of Italian public service television determining "the reproduction of dynamics, dialectics, and contrapositions closer to Parliament than to a corporate" (Leone, Scatassa, 2009: 203).

The bone of contention was the following:

> "It was on March the 14th, Wednesday evening. On RaiDue *Satyricon* was on air (...). Luttazzi calls Travaglio to speak about his book, "The smell of money", four-handed written with Elio Veltri. Unauthorized story of the origins of Berlusconi's economic fortunes, the secret financial mechanisms through which Fininvest was born, the strange arrival in Arcore by the mafia's stableman Vittorio Mangano. Unfiltered television minutes" (Lutra, "Luttazzi e Travaglio assolti. Berlusconi non fu diffamato", *la Repubblica*, 10/20/2005).

Berlusconi was then running for the political election, to take place in two months. Two days after that interview, Michele Santoro focuses the episode of his show *Il raggio verde* on Berlusconi's companies, provoking the intervention of Berlusconi in the show through a phone call, in which he condemned the "real-time trials" Santoro was hosting, instead of providing the public service. Santoro replied "I am working for the public service, not for you, Berlusconi!".[4]

It seems to be a script for this kind of fight:

"The obligation of objectivity in the context of public service media is important because of the scope it gives to those featuring in investigative news stories, especially, to complain about their treatment. More than anyone, it is those in legislative and economic power that can wield the weapon of 'due objectivity' against any public

---

2   www.michelesantoro.it; http://it.wikipedia.org/wiki/Michele_Santoro .
3   "Berlusconi: via Santoro, Biagi e Luttazzi", *Corriere della Sera*, 4/18/2002; see also Rothenberg 2009.
4   http://www.youtube.com/watch?gl=IT&hl=it&v=PgUFclMkPhk, retrieved on 3/21/2012.

service outlet when news coverage becomes commercially or politically inconvenient. The wealthier or more connected they are, the louder they are able to complain" (Higgins, 2008: 11).

Anyway, consequences arrived. As known, Berlusconi sooner after became Prime Minister and pronounced the famous "Bulgarian Diktat". After this event,

> "Michele Santoro and Enzo Biagi, who would both eventually disappear from Italian television for almost five years, became the symbols of Berlusconi's stranglehold on the country's media and what some interpreted as an authoritarian project for Italian society" (Rothenberg, 2009, p. 217).

During this period Santoro was also elected as member of the European Parliament for the left-wing party. Thanks to a judicial decision of reinstatement, he goes back to work in Rai, beginning a new talk show titled *Annozero*. Santoro forms a team with the same correspondent as ever, the journalist Sandro Ruotolo, and three new entries: Marco Travaglio, the cartoonist Vauro and a young journalist, Beatrice Borromeo, as interviewer for the "*Generation Zero*", young people hosted in studio called to express their point of view (Mazzoleni, Sfardini, 2009). *Annozero* has been on the air in RaiDue since 2006, every Thursday in prime time, until June 2011.

In this year Rai announced the cancellation of the contract with Santoro and the major newspapers titled the news as a "*Consensual divorce*".[5] In spite of the wide consensus always expressed by audience rates, Rai decided to cancel *Annozero*, and it was quite impossible not to throw doubt about the possibility of a new attack by Berlusconi to the journalist:

> "It is useless to beat about the bush: *Annozero* had become an obsession for Silvio Berlusconi. (…) This situation is paradoxical, unlikely: any network, anywhere worldwide, would fire one as Santoro. You have to be masochist to pay off a 5 or 6 million spectators per episode show, with peaks of 7 million and over 20% share" (Grasso, "La TV di Stato ha scelto il suicidio. Nessun network licenzierebbe uno così", *Corriere della Sera*, 6/7/2011).

Santoro himself, during the last episode of *Annozero*, commented the event addressing to Rai's President Paolo Garimberti (and his executive board):

> "I have made a deal that ended up the judicial affair, but in this deal it is written in bold: 'Santoro can keep collaborating with Rai' – pay attention, President Garimberti, 'even since tomorrow' – pay attention, colleagues from Rai, 'even since tomorrow'. So then, I would like

---

5   "Santoro-Rai, ora il divorzio è ufficiale. "Rapporto risolto consensualmente", *la Repubblica*, 6/7/2011; "Santoro lascia la Rai: è divorzio", *Corriere della Sera*, 6/7/2011.

you – who is master of your destiny as I am master of mine, but we should be masters of Rai's destiny together, to open this discussion in executive board, and I would like to understand once and for all if you do or do not want a show like this one! I don't want our private talks to be public, because I want to be good with you, but I would like you to take a public stand on it, to discuss it with the board, now that you are free, now that judges are no more at the gate: do or do not you want this show? Because I did not sign with any other broadcaster yet, so since tomorrow, in theory, I could be available to return to this show in the next season at a cost of 1 euro per episode – look Garimberti, in the next season 1 euro per episode (...)".[6]

Santoro's provocation serves the purpose of depicting himself as someone who still cares of public service television, even if expelled, a martyr willing to renounce to his salary if it would be necessary to make the show survive ("we should be masters of Rai's destiny together"). The direct questions he asks to Garimberti and the board seems to be quite rhetoric, implying the unveiling of an hypocritical attitude. Finally, the repetition of "in the next season 1 euro per episode" creates a sort of slogan, as in a (political) campaign.

SERVIZIOPUBBLICO AND THE PUBLIC SERVICE

As predictable, Rai did not give up; the first Italian commercial broadcaster, Mediaset, is in property of Santoro's number one enemy; lastly, he did not find a deal with the second one, La7. Santoro's team needed to find alternative outlets to broadcast their show, and they found it on the Internet.

Santoro and his team announced they were preparing a new show, and asked for the help of the public: they constituted an association, *Serviziopubblico*, whose aim was (and still is) fund-raising. Anyone interested in watching this new show by the brand "Michele Santoro" could donate 10 euro becoming part of this project of crowdfunding.[7] The launch of this project has relied on a call to action video by Michele Santoro, whose words perfectly explain the underlying concept:

"Welcome! Finally we begin. Today our website opens up, and since they often talk about us (not always right), you are going to find here, on our website, news about us. The first

---

6   http://www.rai.tv/dl/RaiTV/programmi/media/ContentItem-61bff9e3-1565-4a9e-91cf-3934944b94a4.html.
7   Crowdfounding or crowdfinancing is the practice of asking the generalized audience to finance a project, typically through the web, as if it was a collective producer. This is more often used in independent movie and web series marketing; see Selva 2010. In the television market it is still an unusual event: in Italy, before *Serviziopubblico*, we can find another project of crowdfinanced television, www.tvpopolare.it, born in 2010 and still active in promoting donations.

news is that on Thursday November the 3rd we are going to be on air wherever it will be possible. They asked me: why don't you try to do it without the public's help? After all, a TV show should stand up on the resources it can find on the market. Yes. But why a program like ours – which last year had so extraordinary results, from the point of view of audience rates, advertising venues, why isn't it on air in Italian television? You know very well what so many people pretend not to know, that is to say in Italy a true market does not exist, nor a true public service. That is why without your help, the public's help, we would have been canceled for a long time from Italian television. The truth is in this moment everyone who could have some doubt that I have left Rai, after what happened to Serena Dandini, after what happened to Roberto Saviano,[8] should better remove all those doubt. Our Constitution, and also the European Charter of Rights, clearly prescribe that governments should not interfere with freedom of expression. On the contrary, this government has done everything it could to stop us peacefully and freely working in Rai – and we also can suppose it have tried to do everything also to prevent us going to work in La7. So, let's say today we are as the Tunisian vendor who is going to sell his fruit and vegetables with his cart, and when they impede him to sell his products he sets himself on fire. We are not going to set ourselves on fire instead – it has to be clear, even if we are going to sell our fruit, our vegetables with our cart, on the Internet, on Sky, and on local TV networks. If someone is going to impede us to do that, this time we are going to keep our cameras turned on, wherever it is possible - in streets, for example, and we are going to keep them turned on until the conflict of interests in this country will be eventually buried. But we could do that only if we are going to have you besides us, our public. For that, I ask you during these hours which are crucial to draw the country's future, and even to draw the television's and media's future, you don't leave us alone. I ask you for 10 euros. And I ask you to extend my request of 10 euro to all your friends, to all your acquaintances, to all your family, even among those who cannot use the Internet, and to whom you have to provide information to do a transfer. Send me 10 euro and keep the receipt, because you will then see how important it is. Your 10 euro will serve to build a little piece of television, without economic owners and without political godfathers. Your 10 euro will be a brick of a house with one only owner: the public, or you. Are we going to succeed? Berlusconi says he has always been a winner, but in reality he has always lost against us. He has lost because he had to use the political power, force, thousands of trick to put us out of play. He has also lost for a fundamental reason: because he does not know the value of the words 'public service'. We have to get a sense of those two words' force: public service. Of those two words' value: public service. And we have to learn up to use those words with all our determination. For that, send me your 10 euro, for the *Serviziopubblico*. Thank you".[9]

---

8 Serena Dandini is an Italian presenter and author, close to the political and intellectual left, whose contract has not been renovated by Rai in 2011, after 30 years of collaboration. This event has been linked to some public statements previously made by the Prime Minister Silvio Berlusconi. Roberto Saviano is a popular writer and journalist, author of a famous inquiry about camorra. In 2010 he co-hosted a successful tv show, *Vieniviaconme*, which it is not sure to be on air again.

9 http://www.youtube.com/watch?v=vwMRU7TmNYk.

It is clear that Santoro is trying to build the credibility of his new show by superimposing the concept of independence (from both political and economic powers), public service and popular share holding. Each one who is willing to contribute to this project will be owner of a little piece of it. Doing this, he states what a public service really means in his opinion: not only the provision of correct, accurate news ("Today our website opens up, and since they often talk about us (not always right), you are going to find here, on our website, news about us"), no matter what this could carry and through which kind of channel ("If someone is going to impede us to do that, this time we are going to keep our cameras turned on, wherever it is possible"), no matter how long it will take for them to resist pressures ("we are going to keep [cameras] turned on until the conflict of interests in this country will be eventually buried"). The public is supposed to be already persuaded that the brand "Michele Santoro" is a guarantee of a good information service: the anchor and his public are united in the unveiling of the hypocrisy of "so many people", pretending not to know that the information system is not reliable in providing news service because the content of what is published is subjected to a political control, responsible of the selection of what can be showed and what cannot ("You know very well what so many people pretend not to know, that is to say in Italy a true market does not exist, nor a true public service. (…) This government has done everything it could to stop us peacefully and freely working in Rai – and we also can suppose it have tried to do everything also to prevent us going to work in La7").

This definition of public service is not enough, because in his opinion a true, radically pure public service also implies the "power of the public" in defining what to watch and what to know. In an interview to a newspaper, Santoro declares:

> "We are relating with an audience who have to look for you through a little effort and a little passion. For that reason, it has to feel represented and partner. (…) A new public, no longer willing to have its own desires and needs massacred by the conflict of interests or by parties" (Truzzi, "Comizi d'amore, Santoro: "Sarà un'impresa". Parte il sito Internet per raccogliere fondi", *Il Fatto Quotidiano*, 10/8/2011).

The power of the public to see "its own desires and needs" satisfied is certified by an economic participation, but this participation to the production of a TV show is mainly symbolic:"your 10 euro will serve to build a little piece of television, without economic owners and without political godfathers. Your 10 euro will be a brick of a house with one only owner: the public, or you. For that, I ask you during these hours which are crucial to draw the country's future, and even to draw the television's and media's future, you don't leave us alone". The independence of the show is guaranteed by the popular ownership, as the first step to build a *res publica* and to establish the basis to maintain it alive in future: the show belongs to the collectivity, and this is an essential requirement to a public service ("We have to get a sense of those two words' force: public service. Of those two words' value: public service. And we have to learn up to use those words with all our determination. For that, send me your 10 euro, for the *Serviziopubblico*").

Santoro embodies such "advocacy role" that Higgins describes as one of the ways in which media assume the political responsibility to serve the interest of the citizenry, which is the soul of any public service medium (Schlesinger, Sorice, 2011):

> "As its legalistic connotations would suggest, the advocacy approach figuratively positions media as the holders of a brief from the political public, and therefore professionally engaged on the public's behalf" (Higgins, 2008, p. 35).

He tells the myth of a popular uprising, whose leader is himself, against political and economic powers, in particular against the Prime Minister Berlusconi ("Are we going to succeed? Berlusconi says he has always been a winner, but in reality he has always lost against us. He has lost because he had to use the political power, force, thousands of trick to put us out of play. He has also lost for a fundamental reason: because he does not know the value of the words 'public service") and embeds this story to the Arab Spring ("today we are as the Tunisian vendor who is going to sell his fruit and vegetables with his cart, and when they impede him to sell his products he sets himself on fire. We are not going to set ourselves on fire instead – it has to be clear, even if we are going to sell our fruit, our vegetables with our cart, on the Internet, on Sky, and on local TV networks").

"ON THE INTERNET, ON SKY, AND ON LOCAL TV NETWORKS"

Serviziopubblico finally made his debut, thanks to the contribution of the newspaper *Il Fatto Quotidiano* (whose deputy-director is Marco Travaglio) and to the donations raised by the public, which at the present moment amount at 1.070.000 euro.[10] The show has been and still is broadcasted on three kinds of screen:

- On the Internet, in live streaming on his official website, Facebook page or YouTube channel, and on two newspaper websites, *Il Fatto Quotidiano* and *Corriere della Sera*;
- On satellite TV, through an all-news channel of Sky;

---

10 http://www.serviziopubblico.it/chisiamo.

- On digital terrestrial television, through local TV networks, whose map is available on the official website, or the national network Cielo (which joined the project later).

Each one of this "screen" represents an alternative medium to the mainstream television,[11] guilty of being subjected to the political control: the Internet because it is perceived as providing a free information, without the government's constraint; the second one because it is the only big competitor for the duopoly Rai-Mediaset (both controlled by the Prime Minister); and the third one, especially local TV networks, because they seem to be close to local citizenry more than national broadcasters. As you can easily have noticed, the reasons of that alternativeness do not lie so much in the technology of broadcasting as in the peculiarity of Italian media system as regards to the complex relationship among media ownership, political power and state institutions (Downey, 2007). The experiment of *Serviziopubblico* has consisted in a mix of usual elements (the host, the team, the format of the show, the themes) with the rhetoric of the attempt to set the information free, challenging the corrupted and arrogant ruling system which would like to exercise a full control on it.

The first episode of *Serviziopubblico* has been opened as usual by a sort of editorial:

> "Dear Enzo Biagi, dear Montanelli,[12] I know you are very worried about me. I know we have been really different from each other but I know you are in this moment watching us with great passion. The truth is we had enough of resisting, resisting, resisting…In my opinion, Monicelli is right: we need to make a revolution. And this is our little revolution: civic, democratic, and peaceful. (…) But I would like to use a very rational argument, and use it just towards those newspapers, and mainly to their readers who follow us, which go on defining me a guru, a prophet, a martyr: I am nothing of that all. I am just a person who tries to be what he is, with his own identity, his own expertise, to act without having owners who oblige us to do what they want(…). This revolution is not partisan: it is not right-sided or left-sided. It is a civic revolution (…). What is interesting is that up against the cancellation of one of our major TV show (however you assess it), the reaction by the information system and also by the party system has been very weak, even by opposition parties! And what happened? 100.000 – I say, 100.000 – people turn the lights of this evening on. Since they turn the lights of this evening on, those 100.000 people making this civic, democratic revolution we are experiencing, can be persuaded that they can turn on everything they want. They can turn on Celentano, they can turn on Daniele Luttazzi, they can turn on Serena Dandini, they finally can turn on Rai, which is slowly turning off, and have a true public service".[13]

---

11 For the definition of the concepts of mainstream and non-mainstream media, see Pasquali, Sorice 2005.
12 Two major Italian journalists, who have been witnesses and protagonists of Italian history since the WWII.
13 http://www.youtube.com/watch?v=v7S2-q5-VQE.

In this last speech Santoro addresses to Italian information system: its conduct is harshly judged because of its silence. Biagi and Montanelli are invoked as spiritual fathers of Italian journalism, who would be very worried about the current state of the freedom of expression. Professionals, who are supposed to be the "power watchdogs", seem to have renounced to this role, to the responsibility towards the general public: a popular revolution appears as the only way to restore the right of the citizens to be informed, which is exactly what a public service means. However, it is not clear who Santoro is addressing to when speaking of the "information system": exception made for television editors (about whom we have already discussed), the two major Italian newspapers in terms of readership, *Corriere della Sera* and *Repubblica*,[14] are in effect supporting his cause, hosting the live streaming on their websites.

Actually, a crisis in traditional journalism credibility (both newspapers and TV news) has been documented in Italy, together with an inverse trend to increasingly trust the Internet as source of news (De Blasio 2010) and SkyTG24 (Sorice 2010). The credibility of Michele Santoro and *Serviziopubblico* is so enforced by his status of outsider from the traditional information system,[15] and also by the promotion of Internet as a counterpart for traditional ways of doing television.

Internet, and in particular social media, have a special role in *Serviziopubblico*'s success[16] also because there was the possibility for the public to write on the Facebook board commenting the episode and asking questions that would have been read during the show. But mainly, the Facebook page was the setting for the launch of some opinion polls: questions were posed to the public, who could answer adding its own option to the list of entries. During the first episode, the first poll was about the most representative persona in the fight against corruption in Italy, and saw the emergence of "nobody" as the preferred option; the second one was a sentence to complete "to bring corruption down we need: …" and the most voted answer was "the revolution!".[17]

Leaving apart for a moment all the considerations about the scientific reliability of the realization of the poll and its results, we have here to highlight the strategic use of the Internet as a symbol for the ability and the "sensitivity" to listen to the voice of the people. The way Santoro stresses the frame of the civic and democratic revolution (and the earlier reference to the Arab Spring) activates a rhetoric which is connected with the common (optimistic) perception and representation of the Internet as a

---

14 www.audipress.it.
15 A similar position is taken by *Il Fatto Quotidiano*, as Peverini 2010 highlights.
16 In terms of audience rates, the mean of the first 5 episodes is 9,63%, corresponding to 2.397.000 viewers; the visits to the only official website have been estimated in 2 millions; http://www.serviziopubblico.it/chisiamo.
17 http://www.facebook.com/servpubblico.

context in which freedom of expression rules above all.[18] In a promotional perspective, this discourse about the Internet is of course functional to the construction of the general frame of resistance to the hegemonic power (embodied by Berlusconi and Rai, and for extension by the whole political and information systems).

CONCLUSIONS

In all the three speeches we have analyzed Santoro chooses whom he is going to address to, as it was a face-to-face conversation: in the first one, he addressed to the president of Rai; in the second one to his public; and in the third one to Biagi and Montanelli. They have the characteristic of activating a frame with a high moral tension: the resistance to the power, the freedom of information and expression, the defense of the public service in its essence of means through which popular participation is possible.

The special care Santoro reserves to his public is the rhetorical way he uses to act as if he was the "advocate" of the people. During this brief essay, we have always talked about "Santoro and his public" because in his speeches Santoro exhibits the relationship he claims to have with it: it is an ideal community who believes in the same ideals and pursues the same goals (freedom of information, representative democracy,…). When in the second speech he speaks about "we" and "you", he makes a proposal for a partnership; then, opening *Serviziopubblico*, that partnership is consolidated and celebrated by the final "And what happened? 100.000 – I say, 100.000 – people turn the lights of this evening on. Since they turn the lights of this evening on, those 100.000 people making this civic, democratic revolution we are experiencing, can be persuaded that they can turn on everything they want". It is as if it was an exhibition of force, in terms of his ability to influence, to involve and to understand people's will (he speaks about "desires and needs"). The reader could have noticed how much this kind of communicative approach is near to populism (Higgins, 2008).

Since credibility is the result of previous and actual relations between the sender and the receiver of a communication (Gili, 2001; 2005), the relationship Santoro is trying to establish with his public relies on four key points, that correspond to the characteristics of a credible source of information:

- Integrity, that is also constituted by the history and the reputation of the source, regarding its moral values such as "dignity, honesty, reliability" and "the specific

---

18   See Lievrouw, Livingstone 2006; Sorice 2009; Lievrouw 2011.

professional ethics" (Gili, 2005: 21). Santoro's dignity and reliability are proven by his history of professional who has always pursued the search for truth no matter what, also suffering dismissal and boycott;

- Independence, or the absence of interest by the source in communicating something that could represent an advantage for itself (ivi: 22). His independence is built upon the exhibition of his neglect for money ("1 euro per episode") and for the establishment's resources ("They asked me: why don't you try to do it without the public's help? After all, a TV show should stand up on the resources it can find on the market. Yes. But why a program like ours – which last year had so extraordinary results, from the point of view of audience rates, advertising venues, why isn't it on air in Italian television? You know very well what so many people pretend not to know, that is to say in Italy a true market does not exist, nor a true public service. That is why without your help, the public's help, we would have been canceled for a long time from Italian television");
- Spontaneity, that is to say the construction of an image of natural, non artificial source: "effects of spontaneity" (ivi: 23) created by Santoro concern the way he chooses to speak to his public, with close-up monologues and a popular language, rich in pauses, interjections, and common saying;
- Homophily, or the real or ideal similarity between the source and the receiver, in order to create a climate of immediate appreciation (ivi: 24). As already noticed, Santoro always tries to depict himself as a member of the people, wondering about why political leaders act like they do, exercising a common critical sense ("those newspapers, and mainly to their readers who follow us, which go on defining me a guru, a prophet, a martyr: I am nothing of that all. I am just a person who tries to be what he is, with his own identity, his own expertise, to act without having owners who oblige us to do what they want").

As we have anticipated, *Serviziopubblico* has built its promotional strategy upon the concept of counter-information, in particular against Rai, as even the name of the show demonstrates. It also supports this concept introducing a rhetoric of participatory journalism:

> "Participatory journalism constitutes a move away from the manufacture of media 'product', and from journalism as an 'expert culture and commodity' (Atton, 2004: 60), toward an interactive, conversational process which, ideally, involves citizens more fully in public life. Participatory journalism thus adopts the *form* of professional journalistic practices and values, but with the *purpose* of challenging and transforming the press as an institution" (Lievrouw, 2011, p. 144).

Reading this definition of participatory journalism, it seems that *Serviziopubblico* can effectively correspond to the model, except for the way people join the journalistic practices: the contribution from the citizens is *de facto* limited to an economic support, because the agenda is defined by the editorial team led by Santoro.

We would need to explore the reception of this show by the audience to know if this communication strategy has worked and persuaded citizens that they were watching a counter-information tv show. In our opinion, it is not sufficient to compute audience rates, web streaming visits and volume of tweets/comments on social media as a signal of victory. In a word, the competition for credibility is still open, and involves not only two subjects, but the concept of public service itself.

REFERENCES

De Blasio, E. (2010). "Informazione e social media. Fra credibilità, fiducia e nuove intermediazioni", in Scandaletti, P., Sorice, M. (eds.). *Yes, Credibility. La precaria credibilità del sistema dei media*. Roma: Ucsi – UniSob – Cdg Editori.

Downey, J. (2007). "Quanto contano la proprietà, le dimensioni e l'internazionalizzazione nell'industria dei media?", in Hesmondalgh, D. (ed.). *Media Production*. Milano: Hoepli.

Gili, G. (2001). *Il problema della manipolazione: peccato originale dei media?* Milano: FrancoAngeli.

– (2005). *Credibilità: quando e perché la comunicazione ha successo*. Soveria Mannelli: Rubbettino.

– (2010). "La credibilità del giornalismo", in Scandaletti, P., Sorice, M. (eds.). *Yes, Credibility. La precaria credibilità del sistema dei media*. Roma: Ucsi – UniSob – Cdg Editori.

Hesmondalgh, D. (ed., 2007). *Media Production*. Milano: Hoepli.

Higgins, M. (2008). *Media and Their Publics*. Maidenhead: Open University Press.

Leone, G., Scatassa, G. (2009). *Economia e Gestione dei Media*. Rome: Luiss University Press.

Lievrouw, L. A. (2011). *Alternative and Activist New Media*. Cambridge: Polity Press.

Lievrouw, L. A., Livingstone, S. (eds., 2006). *The Handbook of New Media*. London: Sage.

Mazzoleni, G., Sfardini, A. (2009). *Politica Pop. Da "Porta a Porta" a "L'Isola dei Famosi"*. Bologna: Il Mulino.

Pasquali, F., Sorice, M. (2005). *Gli (altri) media. Ricerca nazionale sui media non mainstream*. Milano: Vita e Pensiero.

Peverini, P. (2010). "Il Fatto Quotidiano e la ricerca della credibilità", in Scandaletti, P., Sorice, M. (eds.). *Yes, Credibility. La precaria credibilità del sistema dei media*. Roma: Ucsi – UniSob – Cdg Editori.
Rothenberg, N. (2009). "Political cleansing and censorship in public television – a case study of Michele Santoro and Enzo Biagi", in Albertazzi,D.et al. (eds.). *Resisting the Tide: Cultures of Opposition During the Berlusconi Years*. London: Continuum.
Scandaletti, P., Sorice, M. (eds, 2010). *Yes, Credibility. La precaria credibilità del sistema dei media*. Roma: Ucsi – UniSob – Cdg Editori.
Schlesinger, P., Sorice, M. (2011). *The transformation of society and public service broadcasting*. Rome: CMCS Working Paper 2011/01.
Selva, D. (2010). "Open Marketing?", in De Blasio, E., Peverini, P. (eds.). *Open Cinema*. Rome: Edizioni Fondazione Ente dello Spettacolo.
Sorice, M. (2009). *Sociologia dei mass media*. Roma: Carocci.
(2011). *La comunicazione politica*. Roma: Carocci.

OTHER RESOURCES

www.audipress.it
www.corriere.it
"Berlusconi: via Santoro, Biagi e Luttazzi", *Corriere della Sera*, 4/18/2002.
Grasso, A., "La TV di Stato ha scelto il suicidio. Nessun network licenzierebbe uno così", *Corriere della Sera*, 6/7/2011.
"Santoro lascia la Rai: è divorzio", *Corriere della Sera*, 6/7/2011.
www.facebook.com/servpubblico
www.fattoquotidiano.it
Truzzi, S., "Comizi d'amore, Santoro: "Sarà un'impresa". Parte il sito Internet per raccogliere fondi", *Il Fatto Quotidiano*, 10/8/2011.
www.it.wikipedia.org/wiki/Michele_Santoro
www.michelesantoro.it
www.rai.it
www.repubblica.it
Lutra, A., "Luttazzi e Travaglio assolti. Berlusconi non fu diffamato", *la Repubblica*, 10/20/2005.
"Santoro-Rai, ora il divorzio è ufficiale. "Rapporto risolto consensualmente", *la Repubblica*, 6/7/2011.
www.serviziopubblico.it
www.tvpopolare.it
www.youtube.it

Game on the press, between prejudice and technology

Enrico Gandolfi

We have decided to choose the videogame sector inside this book in order to think about the impact of press on digital entertainment texts. Experiential goods, related to a strong market and to powerful technologies, but also to a diffuse prejudice. In the first chapter I will describe the game landscape in numbers and trends, in the second one the game press will be analyzed and then we will see the paradigmatic case of *Rule of Rose* in the Italian context[1].

THE GAME MARKET

The videogame universe is the most important entertainment market in the world, with millions and millions of users; there are a lot of people who consume everyday FPS, MMORPG and social and casual games, but also that use and are influenced by the game culture in populating their fantasies and building their own identity. Gartner estimates that the gaming market in 2011 has reached $74 billion. Parallel to the exponential growth of online and mobile games, the sector with the highest growth rate is the social game one, due to the 'fremium'[2] business model and an heterogeneous audience. The forecasts see the achievement in 2015 of $112 billion, with a strong dominance of digital business. Reuters makes a similar but slightly smaller estimate, with a valuation of $65 billion. For many analysts including Nielsen Group the European market has already surpassed the Asian one in 2008; in Japan software sales decrease of 8%year by year. Europe has always seemed to be more complex to penetrate due the heterogeneity of national contexts and stakeholders, but with the creation of special branches (directly or through coordination) to promote and interact with them, majors are now able to be more present, even in relation to sales

---

1 Articles' translations from Italian to English are by the author.
2 Based on economic microtransitions in game.

charts relatively uniform from country to country. According to DFC Intelligence, Live Gamer and Skrill Holdings the gaming market in Western Europe has reached $ 23 billion and the digital delivery 3.4 billion in 2011, with the expected goal of 7 billion in 2016.

The game industry has a long history and presents various periods; it started in 80's, grew up in 90's and exploded in the last decade. Step by step, the console sector became predominant with the decline of PC one, now very expensive and less served by third parties. By the way, social games and digital delivery are phenomena that have taken attention to this landscape again, also giving possibilities to independent developers to publish their products through portals like Steam or Origin. Nowadays the same consoles have a lot of traits derived by PC world: they are media hub with a minimal overture, and furnish digital delivery platforms.

Today we observe a strong vertical integration in western third party companies, characterized by a 'purism' (expecting Activision Blizzard, possessed by Vivendi Sa): Electronic Arts, Activision Blizzard, Take two, Ubisoft. In Japan in last years there were various fusions following a conglomerate logic. The core products still remain central, but with budgets often hard to sustain. Furthermore, according to Caves (2000), creative industries as the game one are characterized by the "Nobody knows principle" property: consumers' will and movements are unpredictable and not easy to analyze; the uncertainty is a constant, aggravated by the high production costs.

Now minor productions, developed by small teams and usually distributed by digital delivery system, can represent a possible solution for independents but also for big publishers, that can launch new IPs with a kept down risk and pose restored old games again.

In the actual landscape the hardware producers are Nintendo, Sony and Microsoft. The first is the head of the so called 'casual revolution', with the touch (DS) and the movement (Wii) revolutions; the second is the symbol of the popularization of the medium, characterized by a synergic strategy (the game market is functional to others); the third is the protagonist of a rapid rise and a new westernization in console offer. Usually they take profit to royalties paid on each game product for their consoles by third parties, because consoles are usually sold in loss in order to be diffused in the most quickly way. On contrary, Nintendo has chosen the 'interaction front' despite of esthetical one, gaining money from hardware sales and from its own strong brands (from Super Mario to Zelda, with some famous exclusives).

According to the report of the American Entertainment Software Association of 2011, 19% of players spend money on entertainment online play (with a majority given to productions that could be called casual), and 55% play games on their mobile phone. According to this source, the percentage difference between men and women is only 16%. The average age is 37 years, and if we think that the imaginary evocated by the last products and trends is strongly linked to the childhood of this generation, we understand that industry is conscious of that.

Some national markets resist but the internationalization of taste remains high; indeed the Japanese hegemony has left the place to the western one: most important third parties are American, and Japanese creators are now in economic but also creative difficulty, also facing a glorious and heavy past. The expansion to other markets and in all possible platforms is a necessity; a triple-A title costs, and these are the ones that dominate charts; from another perspective this high production risk is able to strongly effect the revenues of a major. According to Ubisoft, PlayStation 3 and Xbox 360 titles require a $ 20/30 million budget, more than the double of the previous generation of consoles. Other analyses have estimated roughly similar. In reality, the costs of platform development, marketing, advertising and location increase the final budget. So the number of copies sold has to be high, usually over a million. Not least the licenses are usually expensive and not so profitable.

The core products based on retail distribution still remain the best business, if we think about hits like Call of Duty, Skyrim, Just dance or Assassin's Creed. The growing dimension of companies and the expansion of the market cause the saturation of products. Butlike in every creative industry, only a small percentage of them generates profits.

Strong brands, sagas and spin-off remain the best manner in which consolidate power and invest money. Charts are dominated by sequels. In the last years, we have assisted to an annually release of the most important brands. A videogame needs 2-3 years to be developed, but with an alternation of teams licenses as Call of Duty or Assassin's creed could be capitalized in the best way. Only majors have the power to risk a new IP, but sometimes it happens and if sales and/or critic response are good the brand will be raised.

If we think about videogame experience, we have to consider that the cost access is considerable, but also the time and dominance ones are high. A game like The Last Story can take dozens of hours and a gameplay training, even if gameplays are less difficult than in the past. Again, the multiplayer side is potential endless and monopolizing. According to the critic response, a lot of good games are flop or not successfully as we can imagine, maybe because an IP better known stoles them attention and money.

I want to use the concepts of 'strategy' and 'tactic' of De Certeau(1984) to go on these studies, and maybe find a like between institutions, texts and audiences according to peculiar contexts.

The first reminds to a comportment inside the common rules, able to win them but in the same hierarchy of values. The second is a sort of resistant act, not organic, that can overturn its context (maybe transforming itself in a strategy). I may employ them looking to the text or going outside it, concerning the cultural industry and the related diffusion of power. From a textual point of view, we have a lot of conduits well established. There exists a strong diorama of recurrent input-output schemes (my "to do" and the manner in which it is transmitted to me) that characterizes the global market. Revolutions in this aspect are less frequent than in graphic one. Now we will propose and indicative categorization in order to better understand what we have written.

- Strategy paradigm: the core text, which sets the tradition and represents a turning point for its genre and generations of players. Often the first chapter of a saga, like GTA, Call of Duty or Assassin's Creed, or something new such World of Warcraft. For some subcultures these videogames enter in a sort of Olympus, essential for their own identity (they symbolize a specific age and a characteristic and maybe vintage way to play); they are the bricks of game culture, linked to the past and delicate to be reformulated (think about the new releases of Syndicate, X-Com or Baldur's Gate).
- Strategy clone: a text, good or bad doesn't mind, that follows another one. The game landscape is full of these products, usually a fashion problem that sees the success, the decline, the death and the resurrection of entire genres.
- Strategy runner: a text that shows a certain grade of openness for the player, what Juul has described as "emergent gameplay"(2005). But all these products remain inside the well known (many ways to arrive to the same end), and this trait is nowadays very common in order to generate hype.
- Strategy shadow: diffused in a hidden way without the main attention of critics and hardcore players; now predominant and often conveying a goal oriented philosophy. It could be the stage before the paradigmatic one. Now we are referring to casual, advertising, social and mobile games, whose products like Angry birds are famous brands.

Videoludic tactics may be text oriented, when I heavily modify a text for innovative goals; there are for example beautiful game art products, UGC with which men have asked their girlfriends to marry them, etc. They can be generated from peculiar strategy texts, but they pretend technical and creative skills. We can translate them in the following categories, that usually don't need a lot of money to be programmed:

- Glorious: a very successful game that remains isolated. A sort of swan without children because its gameplay is too hard to translate, a sort of trouble in reproduction the developing alchemy. Think about Portal, Planescape Torment, etc.

- Serious: serious and activist games that explore delicate topics in order to distinguish themselves to entertainment philosophy. This is an important field in theory, but the production's values are still low and the quality remains various.
- Minimal and key oriented: small productions, one idea based, typical to independent programmers. They can be absorbed by mainstream industry, like Angry Birds, Braid, etc.
- Opposite: the aim of these games is to create resistance and also to criticize something or someone. There are politic and advertising products that try to do that.
- Exotic: interactive texts that look bizarre and strange, both for designer choices and a different culture of provenance, like some Japanese games (No More Heroes, Valkyria Chronicles, etc.). They dependent on the context (maybe in other countries they are strategy).

When a tactical product gains success, maybe becoming a strategy (think about Minecraft), the main industry can absorb it in many ways. One of these are the digital delivery platforms as Steam, PSN, Wiiware and XboxLive: they permit a great diffusion of small profile products, but also consent to majors to impose their will, gain money with revenues and also to recruit with success indie programmers. There is a transformation bridge, in other words a normalization instrument.

As said, usually the entire development process pretends time, money and skilled professionals. Often only big groups can do that, and this explains the strong concentration in videogames market (even if app market and social one make easier the 'garage programming'), where the independent software houses able to compete in world challenge are few, and all more or less linked to big companies.

By the way, gamers show a very heterogeneous nature. They use a lot of different styles of consumption, following stabile trends (like Call of duty's and World of Warcraft's ones) but also giving rewards to indie productions like Minecraft, Torchlight or Limbo. They have a strong liberty in choice products, apparently. There is an enormous variety in market, with a lot of authors, genres and experiences.

Buy the way, the normal user usually doesn't have the time to cross the main directions that the industry and its main competitors indicate. In other words and for a shadow play between majors, the streets that I can walk have well defined traits. Strategies are predominant and not so many (for example the ethnic minorities are stereotyped). We can say that in the modern market they are less than in the past for the bigger production cost. It looks evident to see the redundancy of best game designer products, and also in the number of sequels in development. The indie production, vital and rich, has to fight with these Hollywood style giants, and the domestication of the medium for young generations must touches the hits before arrives to indie ones, more difficult to find and less considered by journalists and media attention. Furthermore, the diffused achievement system in game (a process in which my console monitors my digital activity) can be seen as a sort of intromission in game privacy, and a marketing possibility hard to resist.

But on the contrary there is also a great diffusion of cultists and petty producers (Abercrombie, Longhurst, 1998)in game audiences. Fandom activities and UCG universes are extremely articulated in this field, and the feedback of communities through peculiar gatekeepers it's also fundamental for majors. Think about the public apologies of Peter Molyneux for Fable 3 and of the creators of Dragon Age 2, due to the not excellent level of their products, after the audience reactions; or about the end of Mass Effect 3, about which Electronic Arts, the second third party in the world, was in difficulty.

Despite the decline of PC platform and the growing complexity of engines have slow down the creative community, thanks to the empowerment of portals like Steam and the easier access to programming environments a new and strong independent movement is rising. To sum up, we can individuate in game audiences an extended one (Couldry, 2005) able to elaborate the medial content with great liberty but also dialoguing with a concentrated system that shows peculiars and imperative norms.

GAME PRESS

Videogames are experiential goods, which need a proof in order to be completely accepted. Usually the engagement in a videogame means a lot of hours and a training in order to dominate its system. In the past, demos and shareware versions were very diffused also because the importance of PC as gaming center; even if this practice was possible, the predominance of the console market and the necessary time to build a good sample make it harder (it depends on the genres, some are more difficult to cut). The cost of access is high, if we think that for a console game I have to pay 60-70 euro, and the offer is very rich and heterogeneous. So, gatekeepers and the specialized press have the role to review and to give a fundamental response in order to help consumers.

There is a strong correlation between sales and critic verdict. Aggregator websites like gamerankings.com and metacritic.com are often incorporated in the agreements between publishers and software houses as independent variable for benefits, and very frequently present in financial reports as proof of good performances.

Game critic journalists have a low average age, and often manifest themselves as close to their audience. We are talking about a relatively new medium that relates to an industry still small at the level of experts. In Italy the most of the specialized press is on the web; everyday these portals try to cover all the articulations of the dynamic game world, from cultural issues to guides to consumption: hands on, reviews, news, etc. Even if the main websites are American or English, the production of Italian ones is very impressive and rich, and there is a high frequency information.

In order to furnish a clear categorization that we also will utilize in our case study, we imagine a sort of continuum, from a position dominated by a sporadic attention (external source) to an identity focused on videogame world (insider source), passing to gatekeepers that gravitate around the videoludic medium; these approaches are transversal, in other words there is not a specific type of magazine or website linked to a specific policy about digital entertainment. For example Repubblica.it is a sort of mainstream incubator, but shows a strong attention to the market that we are studying.

We can divide the information sources in:

- Insider: its mission is to treat the game as cultural medium, providing a specialist and expert vision for a typically passionate and informed audience. The reviewers tend to expose themselves and often to become characters and opinion leaders.
- Closer: magazines or portals with a large spectrum of topics, but in which the digital entertainment is permanently present as popular form of culture. The audience can be only interested, maybe enthusiast tourist, otherwise cultist if the main themes are technical of about imaginary. Some mainstream sources have this approach, very flexible in space and in examination given.
- External: sources that cover the medium only occasionally, making it news according to various aims. Not infrequently they are generalist and theatre of medial campaigns. Game market has important numbers and of course also external gatekeepers are interested and sensible about it.

In promoting a product, publishers must clearly relate to these local entities. To the actual saturation we have to add in some national contexts strong prejudice about video games, seen as the symbol of futility and of negative impact on young generations.

It isn't a coincidence that since Commodore 64 era passing by the Nintendo casual revolution this strategy has maintained itself. Adopting the Gramsci concept of 'cultural hegemony', the ludic universe remains a battlefield where economic forces fights with generational and political ones.

There exist some critic parameters in game world well consolidated, searching to catch the most objective judgment. Specialized Journalists have to work with strong analysis categories: gameplay, graphic, longevity, etc. Again, the game generations are very fast and the comparison with other texts is predominant. The graphic state of art, a gameplay that works or a good music are both relative and pure.

In other words, cultural gatekeepers can't escape from this structure too much; of course there are texts able tore verse customs, but they are the exception. In other words the 'infinite variety', typical of creative industries, is not so strong in press' discourses. The reason is that videogames are similar to technical 'products', that have to work efficiently. Bugs, related patches etc. are seen in a very bad way, but the reactions of the community also to not technical problems reveals an engineering vision that limits the freedom of the insider or closer press in giving vote.

A FRAME OVERVIEW

In next pages we will make a synthetic report of the meaning frames about Rule of Rose press cover, in order to identify what ideologies are activated and proposed. We want to investigate the difference between specialized press and generalist one, specifically considering the manners in which these agencies can be exploited or support, even indirectly, digital entertainment texts. Our case study is about Rule of Rose. We chose this game due to two main criteria: firstly it is simply a clone strategy text, similar to its competitors and without innovative issues; secondly the controversy linked to it was, also for the first criteria, extraordinary but at the same time paradigmatic.

For the insider press, we refer mainly to the three websites that, according to the ranking of NetObserver of 2011, were considered the main channels for the game fans: Multiplayer.it (MP) Spaziogames.it (SG) and Gamesurf.it (GS). Such gatekeepers base their legitimacy on the know-how and the reliability of judgment within established parameters.

For the close approach we refer to Repubblica.it, already described, and Puntoinformatico.it, more focused on Informatics and Hi-Tech worlds.

The external perspective of course is the Panorama's one, which has "created" the controversy starting on the physic press and continuing on internet.

RULE OF ROSE - A CASE STUDY

EXTERNAL PRESS

Rule of Rose was a Punch line product published by Sony (in Japan), Atlus (in North America) and 505 Games (in Europe) in 2006, hit by strong controversies and public attacks in Italy and, with less clamor, in other countries.

The weekly magazine Panorama devoted one of its cover, published the November 10th 2006, with the title "Win who buries alive the child". The recalls on the

Panorama website are several and try to perpetuate this perspective; for such reason we will analyze them together. As we will see, the article evokes established frames about the legitimacy of the videoludic medium, but we want to propose a further interpretation, linked to other goals. We only partially trait the crusade against videogame and the mobilization in defense of the new generations, in some ways common in this type of media campaigns.

First of all, for such purposes the instrumental frame on the effectiveness of the game is fundamental: videogames seem to be perfect machines, able to provide a total immersion. But this reveals a derivative promotion and a clear value judgment. What that takes place is the process of 'keying', in which there is a transport of meanings from the dangerous digital potential to the level of the text celebration: Rule of Roses is presented as a high level production, with a realistic aesthetic and a perfect gameplay in its sadism[3]. Again, sexuality seems to be a constant topic, frequent in an interactive experience characterized by every type of perversion:pedophilia, weird homosexuality and so on appear as main issues. As we will see through insider approach there is a strong lack of truthfulness about that: first of all the protagonist is not minor, and this is only the first detail of a long series;again, the journalist, Guido Castellano, doesn't distinguish between cut scenes (not interactive) and in game scenes, and he doesn't write enough about the functional values that the player must follow in order to win, not so perverse. This is a problem if we thing that the interaction is the "fault" and the reason of destructive power of videogames.

"The graphics are so incredibly realistic that Panorama reporter (…) had to turn off the Playstation". (Castellano, November 10th 2006)

"Every single frame exudes perversion. The shots of the girl in the coffin, for example, are taken from the foots, and the camera deliberately lingers on the still immature forms of Jennifer and her skirt, that doesn't stay in its place". (Castellano, November 10th 2006)

"A game that evokes the ogre that might lie in who has the joypad in his own-hands". (Castellano, November 10th 2006)

"That's what shocks: each scene is full of homosexual and sadistic overtones that are not predictable, because the protagonists are not adults but girls". (Castellano, November 10th 2006)

"Jennifer is involved in a succession of indigestible scenes (…). In another situation two little girls holding hands and say softly, 'Princess, you have saved, in return give me a kiss' (…). In a toilet a little girl on her knees licking a finger to her friend sitting on the toilet. While another raises her skirt standing on a sort of altar in front of all the other girls". (Castellano, November 10th 2006)

---

3   Also the images in the main article report cut scenes with details and particulars supporting this description.

As we will see the aesthetics of the game is just average, while some of these scenes simply do not occur. Again, sexuality is surely a sub-theme, but secondary and not so pronounced as it is described. The interactive sessions are very traditional and with fights against monsters.

Another framing act that emerges is the negative educational effect of game and its diffusion, that appears unstoppable. The alleged success of the game is similar to an invincible virus that can touch the 'pruderie' of younger boys, ruining their pure life but already representing a fashion, a prophecy that realizes itself. It's interesting to observe that the game was published in Italy only some days after the article.

"That is sold in thousands of copies. The title, developed by a Nippon software company called Punchline, Japan has been produced and distributed by Sony". (Castellano, November 10th 2006)

"But for all parents, it has little importance, because like it or not Rule of Rose will perhaps also in their houses, released by another label: 505 Games". (Castellano, November 10th 2006)

Now we move on to the bigger and if we want more trivial frame, the one about the status of the videogame as a destabilizing medium, above all able to activate a copycat process more effective than other medial effects. The metaframe in this case it's the conception of ludic as something not serious, futile and in some way dangerous. Related to this we find the discourses about the stances of the Institutions (some famous politicians as Fioroni, Mastella, Veltroni and Frattini) and the possible measures to solve the problem, often ignoring the laws already present; a sort of certification of the magazine's position. A frame that already Entman identifies is the responsibility (1989), which is required both to parents (Veltroni speaks as a dad) and to the same industry, through an embedding process in producers become a reflection of the text, and vice versa.

"The rumor that Rule of Rose has raised at all levels, both in newspapers and in television and also in Parliament, has a bad taste for the industry, probably worried about a possible boomerang effect in Christmas sales". (Castellano, November 20th 2006)

"But also the producers of videogames have a soul. "Leaving a teenager playing with Rule of Rose" admitted (...) Persegati [President of AESVI] "would like to offer a double whiskey". (Marocco, November 28th 2006)

"Producers have very good reasons to react: a turnover in Italy of 741 million and 648 thousand euros in 2005, 16 percent more than last year". (Marocco, November 28th 2006)

The players' community is quoted only once, referring its presumed agreement with Panorama's campaign:

"If some gamers (...) invoking freedom of choice (...), many others have understood the reason of the investigation: put a limit to the violence and to the exaltation of bad values, given to minors". (Anonymous, November 24th 2006).

To summarize what is presented is a rough but effective text, characterized by terrible and indecent themes. The media frame in this case was also implemented by the Institutions that have adopted it, announcing related political actions; broken promises because they are all based on a hypothetical classification system already active under the name of P.E.G.I.. This shows how about some topics the political front is without a frame, and has to link to bigger ones(boys and children without defense, textual and medial responsibility for acts against law and moral and subsequent justification of the irresponsibility of other agencies of socialization and education) that are quite easy to activate in a snow ball effect by journalists/producers.

CLOSER PRESS

Repubblica.it didn't directly deal with the game, but only described the controversy that followed it. This is significant because the game itself doesn't interest the journal , which reveals an equidistant position, which deflates the case and the institutional intent of persecution (Anonymous, November 28th 2006). In the two dedicated articles on Repubblica's website, the journalist lets the fans speak and explain, giving the impression to be neutral and supporting a relativistic perspective.

"But the people of the Net, facing the prospect of a form of censorship, is divided. Even if nobody is willing to attribute exclusively to video games the role of bad teachers". (Gagliardi, November 14th 2006)

"But the sites that specialize in video games such as Tgm online, there are those who remember that it is difficult to see people who go around" wielding chain saws or railgun, running 220km/hour (...) and investing helpless pawns in a mental state of omnipotence". (Gagliardi, November 14th 2006)

Repubblica.it also considers the specialist press, highlighting the deficiencies mentioned above and reporting a rumor about a possible organization top-down from the publisher to have visibility:

"And still the (...) the critics have ruled that Rule of Rose is a mediocre game, and not even with so much (...) violence, a lot of people on the web think that is a programmed case in order to increase the hype and to stimulate the market". (Anonymous, November 28th 2006)

The another portal, Punto-informatico.it, quotes the publisher 505 games when it rejects the arguments of Panorama and signal a strong similarity between the article and a fan review (of the import version) appeared on the website Gamesradar.

it. This possibility could explain the lack of competence showed by the journalist of Panorama.

"505 Games explains that this is not the strategy with which you win the game [referring to bury alive a girl]: 'The burial of the protagonist or of any other child does not appear in any stage of the game, neither indirectly. The scene that sparked this discussion is actually a oniiric sequence that has the function to introduce the game: a non-interactive cut scene in which the protagonist, who is not a minor, is captured inside a tomb'". (Anonymous, November 20th 2006)

"Many posts on blogs refers to accusation appears on GamesRadar.it, in which the article appeared on Panorama would be a copy readapted from an old fan review available online for months". (Anonymous, November 20th 2006)

Following the case in many articles the website shows a neutral conduit, with excellent and heterogeneous declarations but also referring to its community, a skilled one (Anonymous, November 17th 2006). Indeed Punto-informatico.it utilizes the voice of its readers in order to let emerge its position, opposite to the institutional course of action. It's evident that there are some similarities with Repubblica.it.

INSIDER PRESS

The press is unanimous in considering Rule of Rose a mediocre product with a good atmosphere but plagued by a repetitive structure. The puzzles and the sound proposed are however strengths. Votes are 6.9 (MP), 6.5 (GS)and 6.0 (SG). On gamerankings.com the game has a general evaluation of 61,35%, and on metacritic.com of 59/100; a confirmation of the Italian rating.

Examining the reviews on the three insider sites the identification of genre is clear, the survival horror one, of which Rule of Rose is another clone without innovative elements.

"Rule of Rose (...)[is] a Survival-Horror, which is a game where we have to solve a series of puzzles". (Alisonno, January 3rd 2007)

"The gameplay is the one usually offered in every traditional survival horror". (Reina, November 24th 2006)

"The survival horror can be divided into two groups: on one hand we have the psychological ones who bring out our demons, our inner fears (...) stories usually [have] dramatic and disturbing scenes with multiple meanings (...) I start saying that Rule Of Rose definitely belongs to the first category, offering an intriguing and psychological plot". (Buzzi, November 11th 2006)

Again, graphics are not so realistic and beautiful as Panorama has described:

"From this point of view the game deviates from the average quality of 'colleagues': the characters are formed by a discrete number of polygons and texture (...), while the environments in general are stylistically repetitive in some circumstances". (Reina, November 24th 2006)

"Technically, RoR has not particularly valuable items, (...) the realization is at the levelof few years ago". (Alisonno, January 3rd 2007)

"From a purely visual perspective, Rule Of Rose appears in the average of the PS2 games, with characters consisting of a discrete number of polygons and covered with good textures, while the environments received less attention". (Buzzi, November 11th 2006)

Then the verdicts give the image of a minor product, and the absence of sequels it's indicative.

"In general, however, despite the wonderful atmosphere that pervades it and the controversy (...), Rule of Rose is a game designed to be quickly forgotten. It could have been done much more". (Alisonno, January 3rd 2007)

"The plot, based on strong issues, unusual, certainly not" everyday life "in the videogame world, is one of the most intriguing experienced by a video game. The very atmosphere of the game is engaging, urges to play, to see what happens to Jennifer, what lies behind certain situations or murder". (Reina, November 24th 2006)

"Rule Of Rose overlooks the now crowded landscape of survival horror with trying to capture the attention of the themes out of the ordinary. Although the story is intriguing and leads to want to get to the end, the title unfortunately suffers from some problems such as high linearity of the gameplay, which makes it seem like the player to always be "taken in hand" for the continuation of the adventure, not to mention the combat system for review and a certain repetition in level design. "(Buzzi, November 11th 2006)

On MP review there is also an 'outlet' by the reviewer.

"What a game, a movie, whatever stories of certain subjects may divert, disturb the mind of a young man at the point of leading to more or less violent forms of imitation, I think it is sheer demagoguery. Sci. Because a person is influenced by something like this should have his problems. Problems that cannot be searched in the content of certain products" (Reina, November 24th 2006)

It's quite interesting to consider how closer and insider approaches would have simply ignored or merely review Rule of Rose without the attention given by Panorama. External vision has instead brought to the mainstream curiosity a simple clone of Resident Evil and Silent Hill, paradigmatic strategies in skilled views. We don't know if the case has been planned or not, it's hard to say; however, it surely gave benefits to the game from the promotional point of view; talking about it with an 'indirect good response' is better than the silence or only the not excellent verdict of the critics. Looking at the data of Google Trends, there was a strong increase of research on Rule of Rose during November-December 2006, follow by the oblivion.

Again, in a highly competitive market in which the average consumer is well informed (fatherly, survival horror is an 'ascent genre'), the quality is a necessary requirement. At the level of sales we speak about 200000 copies sold worldwide (VGChartz.com data), quite far from a satisfactory result but no so bad for a mere strategy clone. Maybe it sounds banal, but in this sector is so much banal to be significant. Furthermore, from a dark and mysterious land videogames are increasingly known and investigated, and hard to manipulate. They already constitute cultural memories for young adults, not simply toys for children or for 'Peter Pan' men. The fan audience's frame has as parameter the mere value of the text, an issue that Panorama didn't mention. In general it isn't sufficient, but anyway essential. The target for this game is not the fan or the enthusiast, that can play better product buying it only in a period without competitors,but perhaps the same parents or adults who has no parallel frame to propose. This involves a realignment of target in a functional way to publishers.

CONCLUSIONS

To sum up, relying on established frames (ludic as subversive, a vision that wins also against the frame of economic success of the medium, as we have seen considered in a very bad way) to trigger the opening of shadow frames (a textual quality with a shocking plot) can be an effective method to intercept targets more congenial to a peculiar product; people less informed and vaccinated against the medium state of art, without the competence defense also in choosing their gatekeepers. The same game world seems to be a battlefield of ideological but also economical conflict, in which not skilled journalists can be utilized and exploited for assure a certain visibility; the traits of the medium itself, that usually lasts hours and presents strong traditions generationally marked, make the entire game scenario hard to access for 'old' beginners. In other words you can take advantage of sensible elements linked to prejudice in order to provoke a reaction. In the Rule of Rose case this action stimulates what Schudson calls the 'Institutional retention'[4], or a latent version of it, in which the acts of the establishment feed and impose the 'life' of the game on media agenda, mainstream and also specialized; even press not interested is forced to follow it. As we said, the peculiar type of access, the cost of the experience and the generational dominance by

---

4

skilled consumers make this type of operation difficult to execute. Even if interaction would 'corrupt' souls, surely make them more conscious and careful about industry movements, a productive scenario that they fell very close. In the end, playing is much more serious than what appears; indeed who is more vulnerable remains the no player who, after all, can believe to everything.

REFERENCES

Abercrombie N., Longhurst B., (1998) *Audiences: A Sociological Theory of Performance and Imagination*, London: Sage,

Caves R. E., (2000) *Creative Industries: Contracts between Art and Commerce*, Harvard: Harvard University Press.

Couldry N., (2005) *The Extended Audience*, in Gillespie M. (ed.), *Media Audiences*, Maidenhead: Open Uni Press.

De Certeau M., (1984) *The Practice of Everyday Life*, Berkeley: University of California Press.

De Certeau M. (2001) *L'invenzione del quotidiano*, Roma: Edizioni Lavoro (ed. or. 1980) *L'invention du quotidien. 1. Arts de faire*. Paris: Union General d'Editions

Entman R.M., (1989) *Democracy without Citizens*, Oxford: Oxford University Press.

Juul J., (2005) *Half-Real: Video Games between Real Rules and Fictional Worlds*, Boston: The MIT Press.

Schudson M., (1989) *How Culture Works: Perspectives from Media Studies on the Efficacy of Symbols*, in *Theory and Society*, Vol. 18, No. 2.

Sorice M., (2011) *La comunicazione politica*, Roma: Carocci.

PRESS REFERENCES

Alisonno T., *Recensione Rule of Rose*, www.gamesurf.it, January 3nd 2007(http://gamesurf.tiscali.it/dynamic/articolo/CHIAVE/rule4843092108106/TIPO_PAGINA/recensione)

Anonymous, *Nuoviallarmi per Rule of Rose*, www.punto-informatico.it, November 17th 2006 (http://punto-informatico.it/1764592/PI/News/nuovi-allarmi-rule-of-rose.aspx)

Anonymous, *Rule of Rose, ildistributorecontro Panorama*, www.punto-informatico.it, November 20th 2006(http://punto-informatico.it/1769802/PI/News/rule-of-rose-distributore-contro-panorama.aspx)

Anonymous, *Firme contro i videogiochi violenti*, Panorama.it, November 24th 2006 (http://archivio.panorama.it/home/articolo/idA020001038977)

Anonymous, *Videogiochi, la Ue bacchetta l'Italia "No a nuove misure per quelli violenti"*, www.repubblica.it, November 28th 2006 (http://www.repubblica.it/2006/11/sezioni/scuola_e_universita/servizi/videogiochi-violenti/frattini-videogiochi/frattini-videogiochi.html?ref=search)

Buzzi A., *Rule of Rose*, www.spaziogames.com, November 11th 2006 (http://www.spaziogames.it/recensioni_videogiochi/console_playstation_ps2/5531/rule-of-rose.aspx)

Castellano G., *A scuola di ferocia con i videogame*, Panorama (magazine), November 10th 2006.

Castellano G., *Un'Authority per i videogame*, Panorama.it, November 20th 2006 (http://archivio.panorama.it/home/articolo/idA020001038873)

Castellano G., *I videogame violenti nel mirino Ue*, Panorama.it, November 28th 2006 (http://archivio.panorama.it/home/articolo/idA020001039030)

Gagliardi G., *"Bloccare i videogame violenti" e riesplode la polemica*, www.repubblica.it, November 14th 2006 (http://www.repubblica.it/2006/11/sezioni/scuola_e_universita/servizi/videogiochi-violenti/reazione-videogiochi/reazione-videogiochi.html?ref=search)

Marocco T., *Giocatori asociali? Soltanto a metà*, Panorama.it, November 28th 2006 (http://archivio.panorama.it/home/articolo/idA020001039031)

Reina M., *Rule of Rose*, www.multiplayer.it, November 24th 2006 (http://multiplayer.it/giochi/rule-of-rose-per-ps2.html)

Communication Is Business: The Strategic Role of Intangible Assets In The Process of Reputation Building

Mariacristina Sciannamblo

THE ROLE OF COMMUNICATION IN THE REPUTATION BUILDING

The corporate reputation is a huge area including different academic disciplines such as strategic management, organization theory, economics, marketing, public relations and communication. The recent literature about corporate communications highlights the increased importance of the corporate reputation as a strategic agent in the financial performance of an organization (Fombrum & Van Riel, 1997). According to Fombrum & Van Riel,

> "A corporate reputation is a collective representation of a firm's past actions and results that describes the firm's ability to deliver valued outcomes to multiple stakeholders. It gauges a firm's relative standing both internally with employees and externally with its stakeholders, in both its competitive and institutional environments" (p. 10).

Such a definition picks up the contributions of six academic disciplines (economics, marketing, sociology, corporate strategy, organization theory and accounting) that help to find out the multidimensional identity of reputation and its strong connections with some growing key areas of corporate organization such as communications, social responsibility, employee involvement programs, advertising campaigns.

According to Fraser Likely (2006), communication managers not only can measure effectiveness, efficiency and cost-effectiveness, but they can do it on three levels: on the level of product, program and on that of positioning. This kind of framework has deal with the demand of measuring not the "how" (techniques, methods etc.). Rather the "what". Moreover, each level roughly corresponds to communication major roles: technicians, managers and executives. All these figures are involved in the communication programs made up of different products such as media releases, newsletters, speeches, special events, annual reports, webcasts targeted to the same public or audience. All these techniques are set out in the communication plan aiming at the communication effectiveness, which is composed by different effects such as awareness, knowledge, understanding, perceptions, attitudes, opinions and behaviors in different stakeholders. This level of communication effects lead to the area of intangible assets like corporate reputation, corporate brand equity, leadership and relationships. According to Likely, these intangible assets can be seen as "outgrowths" of the previous levels: the cumulative effect of communication outtakes and outcomes that contribute to achieve the desired objectives.

As we have explained, the concept of 'reputation' relates to the effective practice of communications. As remarked by Elliot S. Schreiber (2008), the reputation is founded on values, since they lead the organization to make decisions on what businesses to enter or not to enter, how it treats its employees, whether it fully respects its critics and how it works with its various stakeholders. Corporate communicators, thus, are able to influence values, not just articulate them; so, they earn a growing active role in not only defining the values of the organization, but also in assuring that the values defined are really "first-order" values intrinsic to the organization. In this regard, one of the most important duty of the communication practitioners is the ability to have good relationships with multiple stakeholders. As noticed by James Grunig, the communication area may be the only management function that takes a multi-stakeholder perspective, and this may be one of the distinguishing characteristics of this profession (Grunig, et al., 1999). Moreover, the communication professionals play a pivotal role in managing reputation since they are able to influence the perceptions gained by stakeholders of an organization through a variety of relationships and exchanges. This is the reason why there is a large debate about the need to found out a clear system for measuring the activity of public relations in order to achieve a full legitimacy among the other management disciplines. To date, while there is a general agreement about the strategic importance of measuring communication and reputation performance, there are still some discussions about the measurement topic (Wartick, 2002).

All the company areas concern the three important indicators that composed the performance measurement management framework of an organization: effectiveness, efficiency and cost-effectiveness. According to some studies, the reputation is the best tool trough which it is possible to evaluate the effectiveness of the corporate communication[1]. In fact, the process of reputation building consists in the communication

---

1 As corporate communication we mean the integrative process that aims to build an image coherent with the company identity and with the public perception.

of the same message to the publics, both internal (employees, stakeholders, i.e. share and stock holders) and external (agencies, channel partners, media, government, industry bodies and institutes, educational and general public). It is a coordinated and articulated process that includes a wide range of linguistic codes and styles able to reach any particular audience. Hence, the communication programs gain an important strategic role in defining the articulated relationship between corporate brand, identity and reputation.

As explained by communication scholars, indeed, the brand identity relates to communication strategies, the production and reception of social discourses, the cultural conditions of the circulation of texts, the dynamics of inter subjectivity, the genesis of beliefs and management of trust in people and institutions, and the transformation of collective imagination (Marrone, 2007). Accordingly, a company that succeeds in adapting its identity to the context in which it operates contributes to determine a greater competitive advantage over their competitors. Intangible assets like reputation are indeed valuable, rare, difficult or costly to imitate, substitute and transfer and all these features impede competitive mobility and produce returns to firms.

When the corporate reputation become a strategic asset for the company, the further step is to establish ranking in order to influence stakeholder perceptions of a company's relative value and reputation. The most famous measures of reputation have been developed in the United States and are based on the analysis of brand equity, aiming to find out that reputation have a multidimensional identity. One of the most popular tool to measure corporate reputation is the RepTrak developed by Reputation Institute. This model grounded on four emotional attitudes that stakeholders would have towards companies: Admiration, Trust, Good Feeling and Overall Esteem. According to this conceptual and operational tool, a company's reputation is influenced by seven key elements: Products & Services, Innovation, Workplace, Governance, Citizenship, Leadership and Performance. The RepTrak has been developed through factor analysis with respondents among the general public in a large number of countries. The problematic issues related to its employment concern its focus on the general public. In particular, two problems are underlined: the public may not have familiarity with an organization but still may rate the organization; for many industrial companies, there are many other stakeholders far more important than the general public (Elliot S. Schreiber).

In the next paragraph, we will seek to explain how a famous Italian food industry has reached the lead as the most reputable company on Reputation Institute's Global Reputation Pulse in 2009.

THE FOOD INDUSTRY IS TOP RANKED: THE CASE OF FERRERO COMPANY

In 2009, the Italian company Ferrero moved up to the lead of the Reputation Institute Global Reputation Pulse. According to the Global Reputation Pulse findings, a company's reputation score has a positive and direct link to consumer attitudes and behaviors. Ferrero was the only company that was in the top five on all seven dimensions that drive the ranking: Products/Services, Innovation, Governance, Workplace, Citizenship, Leadership and Performance. The most influential dimension on reputation is Product/Services followed by Governance. However, to earn trust, admiration, good feeling and support companies need to address all seven dimensions of reputation. According to Kasper Nielsen, managing partner of the Reputation Institute, companies that manage their reputation on a single dimension can falter in the negative contingencies; in contrast, companies that manage reputation broadly across several dimensions establish a solid emotional connection with stakeholders that will lead them to support the company both vocally and monetarily in any scenario. The Global Pulse ranking measured in 2009 the corporate reputations of the world's 600 largest companies across 32 countries[2]

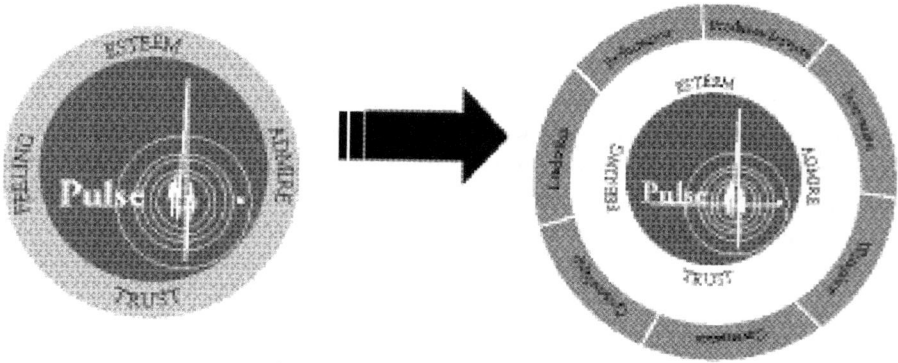

The 2009 Global Pulse Index finds out that Ferrero keep up its leadership in the area of Products and Services, Ethics and Corporate responsibility. It seems to confirm the company's policy inspired by maximum loyalty towards consumers and

---

2   The Global Reputation Pulse 2009 was conducted online in late January and February 2009. A Pulse score is a measure of corporate reputation calculated by averaging perceptions of four indicators obtained from a representative sample of at least 100 local respondents who were familiar with the company. Scores range from a low of 0 to a high of 100, Pulse scores that differ by more than +/-0.5 are significantly different at the 95% confidence level. The mean for all companies included in the study was 64.2.

the trust put in the products[3]. The company practices, in fact, are based on mutual trust between employees, full dedication and transparency towards the group, as well as towards all civil society stakeholders with whom we interact daily. However, one of the best practice in which Ferrero lead is its wise use of communication programs and the consequent advantage for the product positioning and the defining of intangible assets such as reputation, relationships and leadership.

The operation of reputation building, indeed, revolve around an articulated and coordinated visual identity, made up of continuous references to the founding values in Italy and worldwide. This activity is conducted through all the communication products well-integrated according to the different audience and situations: advertising campaigns, public relations, sponsorships, events, packaging.

---

3   http://www.ferrero.com/ferrero-principles/Company-principles/

CORRIERE DELLA SERA

Confronti In classifica anche Pirelli, Eni e Coop. La corsa dei big indiani

La scalata di Ferrero Marchio leader mondiale

Prima per reputazione, sorpassa Ikea

MILANO — Fama e qualità. Questo è ciò che suscita Ferrero nella percezione dei consumatori. Tanto da far salire il colosso della Nutella al primo posto nella classifica delle società con la miglior reputazione al mondo.

Nell'indagine annuale del Reputation Institute, riportata dai siti online dell'Economist e di Forbes, il gruppo di Alba è balzato dal quarto posto al gradino più alto del podio, relegando dietro di sé giganti come Ikea e Johnson & Johnson. Basandosi sulla percezione delle società nei loro paesi d'origine, l'istituto di ricerca (che ha sedi a Copenhagen e New York) ha chiesto al pubblico (con oltre 60mila interviste in 32 Paesi) di classificare i 600 più grandi gruppi al mondo in base a diversi parametri, dalla convenienza e affidabilità dei prodotti alla responsabilità sociale, dalle condizioni di lavoro alla capacità di innovazione. Nonostante l'instabilità economica, il mondo del business riscuote ancora un certo rispetto. Anche se alcuni settori hanno sofferto maggiormente. Le case automobilistiche, al massimo del prestigio negli anni passati, hanno perso molte posizioni: la giapponese Toyota è caduta dal primo posto al cinquantanovesimo, Volkswagen (162 nel 2008) è uscita dalle prime 200 posizioni. Senza contare il settore bancario: l'indice di Ubs per esempio è crollato a 25,14 a fronte di una Ferrero che ha incassato 85,17 (su un totale di 100).

Il made in Italy è presente tra le prime 200 big classificate anche con Pirelli (scesa di una posizione dall'89 al 90), Eni (117) e Coop (dal 94 al 120). Secondo il Reputation Institute da seguire da vicino sono le corporation indiane, le più «virtuose» della lista, con cinque aziende tra le top 50 (solo gli Usa ne hanno 17 ma con cinque volte il numero di company classificate rispetto alle 27 indiane). Fra i Paesi più presenti Francia e Germania, con oltre 30 società selezionate.

Ad Alba festeggiano con il solito understatement e una nota che sottolinea l'«orgoglio» provato per un «tale riconoscimento», «uno straordinario tributo a tutti i collaboratori di Ferrero che si impegnano quotidianamente per la qualità. «Ma è anche un successo dell'industria italiana nel mondo», conclude la nota del gruppo piemontese, guidato dalla terza generazione dei Ferrero, Pietro e Giovanni.

Antonia Jacchia

July 5th 2012

Ferrero stands out for a consumer-oriented communication strategy together with a business strategy founded on the uniqueness of its products. The best example in this sense is Nutella, the popular hazelnut cream created in the 1964 by Michele Ferrero, the son of the founder of the Ferrero company, and now sold in over 75 countries[4]. Nutella, together with the Kinder products, is the product the embody the company consumer-oriented strategy which is based on long-standing and mutual trust. The communication with consumers is built on a proper use of the products and on the promotion of healthy lifestyle; it is not a coincidence, therefore, that the communication policies affects the promotion of the sport through various initiatives such as, for instance, "Kinderiadi" and various forms of sponsorship in national and international sports events.

---

4   http://www.nutellausa.com/history.htm

May 8th 2012

The promotion of healthy lifestyles among children and young generations by encouraging the practice of physical activity and daily sport is connected to the attention in the selection of quality raw materials, sourced in full respect of a strict ethical code concerning their origin, harvesting and manufacturing. In a global context of growing attention to themes such as nutrition and wellness, the focus of the research strategy and production investments is on the creation of high quality products, carefully developed in terms of their nutritional value and portioning, so that they can be integrated into a balanced diet, with particular attention to the needs of children and families.

CONCLUSION

Observing the communication and business strategies laid on by Ferrero, we can notice that they are focused on the perceptions of different stakeholders. These perceptions are organized into mental frameworks shared by the stakeholders in the relational networks in which they are include (Romenti, 2008). The studies in the field of marketing and social psychology underlined the role of the relational networks of stakeholders related to the development of reputation. As several theorists have remarked, the corporate reputation is the result of process of socialization and sharing within these network of relationships (Fombrun et al., 2000). In this regard, reputation may be conceived as the system of different meanings attributed to the choice made by the firm and to the choices relating to the corporate identity. In order to develop a strong reputation, it become pivotal to adopt different kind of communication strategies: on the one side, the disclosure of information that serves to increase the visibility of corporate behavior and its distinctive features, on the other the choice to set up a symbolic and narrative communication that enhances the transparency of the company and ensuring coherence between messages conveyed inside and outside (Romenti, 2008).

By supporting a strong attention to the products, production process and procedures, the Ferrero Group demonstrates to maintain its focus on Product and Service in order to improve its own reputation, but, in the same time, it seems to be more engaged in developing communication programs related to others specific drivers of the Global Pulse: Citizenship, Innovation and Governance. To improve its citizenship, the company are committed in developing several initiative in the field of corporate social responsibility. In 2011, the Group adopted the Code of Business Conduct, aiming to share with its suppliers, trade partners, commercial agents, subcontractors, distributors, vendors and their employees, the Ferrero principles as well as the high Ferrero standards on excellence of its products. It is based on five priorities[5]: excellence of product quality and safety, human rights commitment, environmental protection and sustainability, conditions of workplace environment and business integrity. This document operates in compliance with the Ferrero Code of Ethics, which is helpful to keep the spotlight on the company's guiding principle within the entrepreneurial objectives[6].

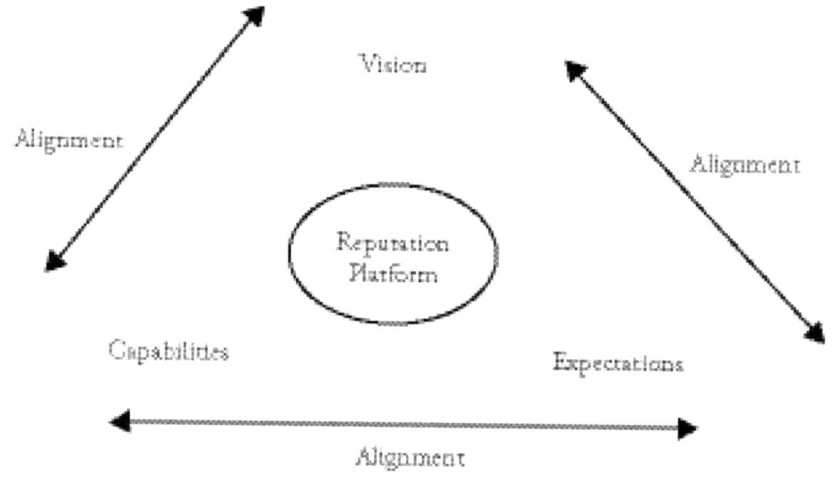

---

5   http://www.ferrero.com/social-responsibility/code-business-conduct/
6   http://www.ferrero.com/social-responsibility/code-of-ethics/reliability-trust/

As far as governance is concerned, it is strictly related to the stakeholder relationship management aiming at defining the most relevant stakeholder for the company and setting up the best relational and communication strategies most suitable to reach them. As Stefania Romenti have remarked, reputation is one of the indicators for the success of the model governance adopted as it is "born" and "evolves through" the quality of interactions between the firm and its stakeholders. Moreover, reputation is able to strengthen the value generated by the company because it influences the propensity of economic actors to offer or deny their support to the company. Hence, according to this approach, the reputation is conceived along an ideal path that start from the strategic foundation of the company and ends with its tactical execution. The company vision embodies its core values, mission and its desired reputation; it leads to the reputation platform which regards the alignment between the company's vision, its capabilities to implement it and the expectations of stakeholders.

This framework needs to be implemented through a reputation strategy and the consequent reputing initiatives. Goals, governance and processes are to be established together with the technical tools. In the first place, it will be essential to listen the the needs and expectations of stakeholders to understand what issues may affect their perceptions about the business. This is done through continuous activities of dialogue and mutual understanding between the company and its stakeholders. Secondly, it will be need to translate the results of listening in a distinctive identity and responsible behavior, or in decision-making and managerial (Invernizzi, 2002). Then, it should build communication programs that spell out the company identity and that make its behaviors clear. Accordingly, both the activities of listening and the communicational and relational ones are essential for developing a good reputation related to the company's stakeholders.

A further step towards a more active involvement of the relationships in the processes of decision-making will be the stakeholder engagement besides the relationships management, in the pursuit of common goals and solid bridges between the company and its critical resources (Invernizzi, 2002).

REFERENCES

Fombrün, C., Van Riel, C. (1997). The reputational landscape. *Corporate Reputation Review* (1997) 1, 5–13. http://www.palgrave-journals.com/crr/journal/v1/n1/abs/1540008a.html.

Fombrun C.J., Gardberg N.A., Sever J.M. (2000). The Reputation Quotient: a Multi-Stakeholder Measure of Corporate Reputation. *The Journal of Brand Man-*

agement, vol. 7, n. 4. http://www.mendeley.com/research/reputation-quotient-multistakeholder-measure-corporate-reputation/

Grunig, J.E., Hon, L., Childers, L. (1999). Guidelines for measuring relationships in public relations. *Institute for Public Relations.* http://www.instituteforpr.org/topics/measuring-relationships/

Invernizzi, E. (2002). La poliedricità della comunicazione per lo sviluppo dell'impresa. *Sinergie : periodico di studi e ricerche,* n. 59, p. 19-38.

Likely, F. (2006). Communication and PR: made to measure. *Institute for Public Relations.* http://www.instituteforpr.org/topics/communication-and-pr-made-to-measure/

Marrone, G. (2007). Il discorso di marca. Modelli semiotici per il branding. Laterza.

Romenti, S. (2008). Corporate governance e reputazione: dallo stakeholder relationship management allo stakeholder engagement. *Impresa Progetto Electronic Journal of Management,* n. 2.

Schreiber, E. S. (2008). Reputation. *Institute for Public Relations.* http://www.instituteforpr.org/topics/reputation/

Wartick, S. L. (2002). Measuring corporate reputation. *Business & Society,* 41, 371-392. http://bas.sagepub.com/content/41/4/371.abstract

www.ingramcontent.com/pod-product-compliance
Lightning Source LLC
Chambersburg PA
CBHW051107160426
43193CB00010B/1350